Life Coaching

A Cognitive-Behavioural Approach

Michael Neenan and Windy Dryden

Routledge
Taylor & Francis Group

LONDON AND NEW YORK

First published 2002 by Routledge
27 Church Road, Hove, East Sussex BN3 2FA

Simultaneously published in the USA and Canada
by Taylor & Francis Inc.
270 Madison Avenue, New York NY 10016

Reprinted 2002, 2003, 2005, 2006 and 2008

Routledge is an imprint of the Taylor & Francis Group, an Informa business

© 2002 Michael Neenan and Windy Dryden

Typeset in Times by Mayhew Typesetting, Rhayader, Powys
Printed and bound in Great Britain by TJ International Ltd,
Padstow, Cornwall
Cover design by Sandra Heath
Cover illustration by Nick Osborn

This publication has been produced with paper manufactured to strict
environmental standards and with pulp derived from sustainable forests.

British Library Cataloguing in Publication Data
A catalogue record for this book is available from the British Library

Library of Congress Cataloging-in-Publication Data
A catalog record for this book is available from the Library of Congress

ISBN13: 978-1-58391-138-9

Contents

Acknowledgement

We wish to thank *Counselling*, the Journal of the British Association for Counselling, for permission to reprint material contained in Chapters 3 and 7.

Preface

The way you think about events in your life profoundly influences the way you feel about them; change the way you think and this will, in turn, change the way you feel. This is the essence of a widely practised and research-based counselling approach called cognitive-behaviour therapy (CBT). Understanding your view of events provides the insight into why you feel and act in the ways that you do (e.g. you are anxious about public speaking and avoid it because you fear that your performance will be less than perfect). Armed with this knowledge, you can then decide if you want to change this viewpoint in favour of one that is more likely to bring you better results in life (e.g. 'Competence and confidence will come through actually doing it. Doing it as well as I can is far more important than doing it perfectly'). How this is achieved is the subject of this book.

The founders of CBT, Aaron Beck and Albert Ellis, have been very keen to move it out of the counselling room and into the wider society in order to reach the largest audience possible with their problem-solving or psychoeducational methods. We are particularly interested in its psychoeducational aspects in our work with non-clinical groups and call our practice in this context cognitive-behavioural coaching (CBC). Coaching has been defined as 'the art of facilitating the performance, learning and development of another' (Downey, 1999: 15). We believe that CBC fits the bill for such personal growth.

CBC does not offer any quick fixes to achieve personal change or 'magic away' personal difficulties; it does emphasize that sustained effort and commitment are required for a successful outcome to your life challenges or difficulties. So if you are the kind of person who wants great change for little effort, then this is not the book for you! Remember that it is not just reading a self-help book that changes you but the amount of hard work you expend on putting into daily practice what the book recommends.

Who is this book for? Well, it is aimed at that neglected species in this 'dumbing down' age, the intelligent reader. This person keeps her critical faculties sharp by engaging with new ideas, welcomes opposing viewpoints, is unafraid to change her mind and seeks opportunities for self-development. However, even these fine qualities cannot prevent you from underperforming or becoming stuck in certain areas of your life.

In this book then, we look at some common difficulties such as procrastination, unassertiveness, poor time management, not dealing constructively with criticism and lacking persistence in the pursuit of your goals. If the information contained within these ten chapters is absorbed and acted upon, you will find that increased personal effectiveness leads to a more productive and satisfying life.

Chapter 1

Dealing with troublesome emotions

INTRODUCTION

Samantha enjoyed her job as a sales rep and had worked for the same company for five years. Despite her considerable experience in the job, she still felt intense bouts of anxiety when giving presentations or meeting new and important customers: 'This should not be happening to me after five years in the job.' Raymond liked to see himself as calm and cool under pressure, a man who took problems in his stride but, unfortunately, his persona did not always reflect reality – he often flew into a rage if, for example, he could not find his car keys or assembling DIY furniture proved too complicated: 'Why do I behave like that? Why can't I control myself?' Janet had to get a full-time job to make ends meet and therefore had to find a childminder for her two children. Even though she knew they were being well looked after, she still felt guilty about 'abandoning' them: 'I should be there to pick them up from school and give them their tea.' Brian could be clumsy sometimes and felt hurt when some of his friends laughed at him for tripping over his own feet or bumping into things: 'It's not fair when they laugh at me. I can't help being uncoordinated.' In each of these four cases, the emotions prove troublesome because though not incapacitating or requiring professional attention, they nevertheless hover in the background, unresolved and ready to intrude again.

When I (MN) asked each person what caused their troublesome emotions, they said, respectively, giving presentations and meeting important customers, searching for car keys and doing DIY, having to go to work and leaving her children with someone else, and being laughed at for acting clumsily. In other words, external events or others create their feelings. While this view of emotional causation is a popular one – count how many times in the next week you or a friend says something like 'He/she/it makes me feel this way' – this does not mean it is an accurate one. The most important part in the chain of emotional causation has been left out – yourself! In order to experience an emotional reaction to an event, you first have to evaluate the personal significance of the event. An American psychologist, Dr Albert Ellis, uses a simple model to show how we largely upset ourselves about unpleasant events in our lives:

A = activating event – the end of a relationship
B = beliefs or thoughts – 'Without her, I'm worthless'
C = emotional and behavioural consequences – depression and withdrawal from social activity

Initially, you might say that A caused C ('Who wouldn't be depressed if their partner left them?'). This viewpoint overlooks individual variations to the same event, i.e. not everyone would feel depressed about the end of a relationship: one person might be anxious about coping alone, another might feel angry at being dumped, a third person feels relieved that it is over while a fourth feels ashamed that he did not fight harder to preserve the relationship. Therefore, in order to understand C you need to focus on B, not A. You might get angry at this point (what are you telling yourself?) because you think we are minimizing or paying no attention to bad events in people's lives. Not so. Events at A can contribute powerfully to your emotional problems but your beliefs and thoughts at B ultimately determine how you feel at C. We will use an extreme example to illustrate this point. Viktor Frankl, an eminent psychiatrist who died in 1997, was spared the gas chambers at Auschwitz and put to work in the camp, enduring hideous suffering, but never losing hope. He observed that 'everything can be taken from a man but one thing: the last of the human freedoms – to choose one's attitude in any given circumstances, to choose one's own way' (1985: 86).

Whatever the situation, you can choose how you wish to react to it because you do have some measure of free will. Events, whether past or present, do not impose their feelings on you; your feelings are largely determined by your attitudes to these events. In other words: *you feel as you think* (Burns, 1981; Dryden and Gordon, 1991).

ANTS IN YOUR MIND

When you are feeling bad (e.g. angry), ask yourself: 'What is going through my mind at this moment?' in order to tune into what are called automatic negative thoughts (ANTS; Beck, 1976). These thoughts are called automatic because they pop into your mind involuntarily and therefore are not the product of reflection or reasoning, seem plausible at the time of their occurrence and are difficult to 'turn off' (ANTS can also be images, daydreams and fantasies). Two examples:

(1) your partner is late coming home and you feel anxious because your mind is flooded with disturbing thoughts (e.g. 'What if he's been involved in a pile-up or hit by a drunk driver?') and images (e.g. trapped in the burning wreckage). He eventually arrives home safe and you now feel relieved because you are able to 'turn off' the anxiety-provoking thoughts and images by telling yourself 'There was nothing to worry about after all'.

(2) you see your wife in the high street talking to and embracing another man and immediately feel jealous: 'Who the hell is that? Why are they laughing so much? They're having an affair. She's planning to leave me.' When she gets home, you interrogate her and discover it is her brother whom she has not seen for several years. You now feel ashamed because you are thinking: 'I'm so stupid for jumping to conclusions. I've shown my wife how jealous and insecure I am.'

In order to change the way you feel, you need to change the way you think; added to the ABC model are D and E. D is for disputing or questioning your upsetting thinking. When you are emotionally upset your system of thinking usually becomes closed and disputing questions help to change it back into an open system (e.g. 'Where's the evidence that I'm worthless?'; 'How will believing I'm worthless help me to find another relationship?' 'Would I call my best friend worthless if her relationship ended?'). Disputing employs the technique of decentring whereby you stand back from your upsetting thinking and examine it in a realistic way (Blackburn and and Davidson, 1995).

We would suggest that a lot of your emotional difficulties are largely self-defined, i.e. you define your difficulties in a way that leads to emotional trouble. For example, you imagine that making a mistake in front of others would be a disaster instead of a setback (anxiety); smacking your child means you are a wicked mother rather than a mother who had a momentary loss of control (guilt); if others discover you are dyslexic, then this would expose you as an idiot instead of someone who has difficulties with reading and spelling (shame). Through disputing or thinking about your thinking in more helpful ways by using reason and logic, you can learn to develop an effective (E) outlook that promotes greater emotional and behavioural stability in your life.

When you are questioning your thinking, you are acting as a personal scientist, i.e. treating your ideas and beliefs as hypotheses rather than facts and reality-testing them in order to find alternative explanations and behaviours that are more helpful in solving your emotional problems. Typical questions to ask yourself in order to challenge your ANTS include:

- Is the thought true? If it is, what is the worst that can happen and could I cope with it?
- Which distortions are present in my thinking? (see below).
- If my friend had the same problem as me, would I judge her as harshly as I judge myself? If the answer is 'no', then what makes me so different? What advice would I offer her that I am not prepared to follow myself?
- What is the evidence for and against this thought?
- Are there other explanations for the situation that are more reasonable or realistic?
- Would a jury agree with my interpretation of events? If not, what evidence might they use, which I have overlooked, in order to arrive at a more accurate appraisal of the situation?
- What are the short-term and long-term advantages and disadvantages of holding onto this thought?
- How might things look in three or six months' time?
- If others do see me in a negative way, do I have to agree with them? If I do agree, then what evidence do I have for my negative appraisal?
- Am I giving equal weight to the positive and negative factors in this situation or am I focusing only on the negative ones?
- Am I judging myself on the basis of my actions? Can my actions ever truly and totally define me?
- What steps would I need to take to determine if this thought is true or false?

- Even though the evidence continually points to the thought being inaccurate, what prevents me from believing the evidence?
- Does this thought help or hinder goal attainment?

DISTORTED THINKING

When we are emotionally upset, we often process incoming information in a consistently biased and distorted way that maintains our low mood, angry behaviour or anxious state. Some of the common distortions (also known as thinking traps) found in emotional problems include:

- All-or-nothing thinking: seeing events in extreme terms that allows for no shades of grey or middle ground, e.g. 'If I can't have her, then no one else will do'. The antidote to this kind of thinking is balanced, non-extreme appraisals of a situation that allow you more options to choose from, e.g. 'She would be the ideal partner but I'm sure that I can be happy with other women'.

- Magnification/minimization: exaggerating the negative and reducing the positive (e.g. 'I stumbled over a sentence and turned the talk into a disaster' and 'Some people said they enjoyed the talk but what do they know?'). What is required from you in tackling these distortions is a sense of proportion (e.g. 'Stumbling over a sentence was a just hiccup and the rest of the talk proceeded smoothly' and 'Some people enjoyed the talk which indicates that it went reasonably well').

- Personalization: holding yourself to blame for events you are not responsible for, e.g. 'I made my wife have an affair'. With this distortion, it is important to distinguish between your actual and presumed responsibility for an event, e.g. you have contributed to marital discord by working long hours at the office but your wife chose to have an affair to satisfy her needs.

- Emotional reasoning: you believe something is true because you feel it strongly, e.g. 'I feel like a failure, so I must be one'. Feelings are not facts or reflect objective reality; so it is important to examine evidence dispassionately in order to arrive at an accurate assessment of the situation, e.g. 'It is true that I've had some recent failures but they don't make me a failure as a person. The part does not define the whole.' As Gilbert observes: 'When we use feelings to do the work of our rational minds, we are liable to get into trouble' (1997: 93).

• Mind-reading: the ability to know the thoughts of others without using the normal means of communication, e.g. 'My boss doesn't say, but I know he thinks I'm an idiot'. Often, negative thoughts such as these are in your mind and therefore you imagine they must also be in the minds of others. Instead of mind-reading, ask the other person or wait until you have firm evidence to support your beliefs. If you did ask your boss and he denied thinking you were an idiot and you did not believe him, you have gone back to mind-reading!

• Labelling: you attach a global and negative label to yourself based on specific behaviours, e.g. 'I failed to pass the exam, so that makes me a moron'. Here you are assuming your behaviour reflects your totality as a complex and fallible (imperfect) human being. As Leahy succinctly asks: 'Is it a behavior that fails or the entire person?' (1996: 99). If you want to use labels, then attach them to your behaviour instead of yourself, e.g. 'I failed the exam but that certainly does not make me a moron'. Focusing on behaviour change (e.g. 'What can I do to help me pass the exam at the second attempt?') is more constructive than the consequences of self-condemnation (e.g. 'As I'm a moron, there is no point whatsoever in attempting the exam again and bringing more disgrace on myself').

• Discounting the positive: any positive experiences or qualities are disregarded, e.g. 'People say the workshop was a success but they are just trying to make me feel better because they know it was a failure'. Discounting the positive will make your life seem relentlessly one-sided and maintain your low mood. Including the positive as well as the negative will lead to a more balanced assessment of your present difficulties (e.g. 'Certainly the workshop had its flaws, but I very much doubt that these people are all banding together to lie to me').

• Shoulds and musts: these are usually in the form of rigid rules of living that you impose on yourself, others and/or life (e.g. 'I must never show any weaknesses'; 'You should always give me what I want'; 'I must not have too much pressure in my life').

When these rules are not obeyed, you will often condemn yourself (e.g. 'I'm spineless'), others (e.g. 'You bastard') or life (e.g. 'I hate this stinking world'). Rigid musts and shoulds make you subservient to a totalitarian system of thinking. The alternative to rigid rules are flexible ones which allow you to acknowledge and act in accordance with the reality that yourself, others and/or the world rarely fit with how things must or should be.

- Mental filter: focusing exclusively on one negative aspect of a situation and thereby judging the whole situation by it (e.g. 'I knocked over a glass of wine and the whole evening was a disaster because of it'). Burns memorably likens mental filtering to 'the drop of ink that discolors the entire beaker of water' (1981: 40). Instead of dwelling on one aspect of the situation, stand back and view the whole situation in an objective way (e.g. 'Spilling the wine did lead to some embarrassment on my part and some irritation on theirs, but once that was over, we all seemed to have had a pretty good time').

- Fortune-telling: believing you can predict the future in a consistently accurate way. While you probably do make some accurate predictions (e.g. 'This new job is going to entail a lot of hard work and responsibility') others will be wide of the mark, particularly when you are in a pessimistic or negative frame of mind (e.g. 'I failed my driving test. I'll never be able to pass it'). You may consider that your predictions are 'accurate' because you act in a way that makes them come true (e.g. you predict you will not be able to give up smoking, so when you try to, you start feeling irritable and moody; instead of tolerating these feelings as part of the withdrawal symptoms, you conclude that you cannot cope with them and resume smoking). One way to assess how good a fortune-teller you are is to write down some of your predictions and review them objectively in a few months' time to determine how accurate they are.

- Overgeneralization: drawing sweeping conclusions based on a single event or insufficient information (e.g. 'Because my relationship has ended, I'll never find anyone else and I will always be unhappy'). Overgeneralization can be brought under control by examining what evidence you have for your sweeping conclusions and advancing alternative arguments in the light of it (e.g. 'My relationship has ended and it will be hard to find another partner if all I do is mope about at home, but I'm more likely to find some-one else and have some happiness if I start to socialize again').

- Catastrophizing: always assuming the worst and, if it occurs, your inability to cope with it (e.g. 'I'm sure my boyfriend is going to dump me because he doesn't phone me as much as he used to. If he dumps me, I'll completely fall apart and never get over the rejection'). McKay *et al.* state that 'there are no limits to a really fertile catastrophic imagination' (1997: 30). Challenging catastro-phizing involves, among other things, asking what is the probable outcome versus the possible outcome? In the above example, the probable outcome might be that the person is not going to be 'dumped' but the relationship is going through a difficult period. On the other hand, the possible outcome might be rejection and therefore the person needs to learn how to adapt constructively to this grim reality in order to tolerate rejection and not fall apart (decatastrophizing). It is important that you learn to play the odds more accurately (Warren and Zgourides, 1991), e.g. how many of your catastrophic predictions have actually been realized? (possible answer: one). Next time you catastrophize, remember the odds that it is highly unlikely that the dreaded outcome will occur.

CORE BELIEFS

The distortions in thinking outlined in the previous section fre-quently stem from underlying negative core beliefs which are usually formed earlier in your life (e.g. childhood or early adoles-cence) and are activated from their dormant state when you are upset (we like to see these core beliefs as 'light sleepers'). Core beliefs are global and absolute (e.g. 'I'm incompetent'; 'Nobody can be trusted'). Once active, these beliefs pass into your awareness and determine how you will view a situation. For example, you are passed over for promotion and become depressed because you believe 'I'm not good enough' and you now question whether there is anything good in your life. Once the emotional crisis has passed, the belief returns to its dormant state but ready to be reactivated at a later date unless this belief is modified or changed in some way. Negative core beliefs leave you vulnerable to future episodes of emotional misery. To uncover core beliefs, you can use a technique known as the downward arrow which follows the personal implications of a hot (i.e. emotionally charged) automatic negative thought by asking for the meaning of each thought revealed (Burns, 1981, 1989). For example, Jane was anxious about attending a party because she thought:

'I won't get off with anyone'
    ↓   If that's true, what will that mean to me?
'That I'll go home alone'
    ↓   If that's true, what will that mean to me?
'No one fancies me'
    ↓   If that's true, what will that mean to me?
'If no one fancies me, then I'll be all alone' (underlying assumption)
    ↓   If that's true, what will that mean about me?
'That I'm undesirable' (core belief)

Asking yourself what a thought means *to* you often reveals an underlying assumption which is identified by an 'if . . . then' construction; asking what it means *about* you usually reveals a core belief (Beck, 1995). When you are using the downward arrow technique, assume temporarily that each thought is true in order to concentrate your mind on revealing a core belief. If you disrupt this technique by challenging each thought (e.g. 'Do I always go home alone?') you will probably prevent yourself from reaching the 'bottom line [core belief]' (Fennell, 1997).

Once a core belief is revealed, you can ask yourself the same questions and identify the distortions in your thinking as described above (e.g. 'How does not getting off with someone at a party mean I'm undesirable?'; 'I'm using labelling and all-or-nothing thinking'). If Jane wants to change her view of herself as undesirable, then how would she like to see herself? She said 'desirable' but this self-image was a balanced one, i.e. it incorporated 'getting off with someone' as well as rejection and indifference to her. Her concept of desirability was a flexible one and able to provide more emotional resilience in times of loneliness whereas her concept of undesirability was an inflexible one leading to prolonged bouts of unhappiness.

To reinforce her new self-image, Jane went through her life to find historical evidence to support it (e.g. boyfriends, marriage, affairs) and kept a diary for several months to collect current evidence (e.g. being chatted up, a few dates, hearing that 'someone fancies me'). Also, Jane conducted an analysis of the development of her 'undesirability' self-image (e.g. 'I always thought that if someone I fancied didn't fancy me then I was undesirable. I realise now how simplistic that was') to provide herself with a map in order to understand how she got from 'there to here' (Scott *et al.*, 1995). When Jane's new self-image 'collapsed' or was 'shaken' from time to time, this usually meant that she had reverted temporarily to believing she was undesirable (e.g. someone she fancied did not reciprocate) and started examining the evidence again to confirm or disconfirm this conclusion. In this way, the ideas underpinning her old self-image were gradually weakened while the ideas supporting her new self-image were gradually strengthened.

SOME COMMON TROUBLESOME EMOTIONS

In this section, as well as describing the main features of these emotions, we also provide additional techniques for dealing with them.

Anxiety

Anxiety is based on future-orientated thinking that encompasses themes of danger or threat where you will be vulnerable in some way. People frequently overestimate the dangerousness of a given situation and underestimate their ability to cope with it. The threat or danger can be viewed along a continuum of time from imminent ('Oh my God! I'm going to pass out'), to the near future (e.g. 'I know I'll show myself up when I meet my husband's friends this weekend') and longer-term (e.g. 'I'm sure this lump on my shoulder is going to prove cancerous in a couple of years' time'). When you are anxious you may experience some of the following symptoms: breathlessness, palpitations, trembling, sweating, dizziness, hot flushes, 'jelly legs'. These symptoms are the same for a physical danger (e.g. a burglar in your house) as for a psychosocial threat (e.g. fear of rejection). Depending on your evaluation of the situation you might strike out (fight), escape the situation (flight), become immobilized (freeze) or collapse (faint).

Fear can be distinguished from anxiety: the former is an appraisal of a perceived threatening stimulus (e.g. 'I know I'm going to freeze in front of all those people when I start my presentation and look a complete idiot') and the latter is the emotional response to the appraisal (Beck *et al.*, 1985). When you feel anxious you may try to avoid or withdraw from the threatening situation or seek reassurance from others that the feared outcome will not occur. This behavioural strategy provides short-term relief from anxiety but reinforces it in the long term. When you are anxious you will often engage in 'What if . . .?' thinking (e.g. 'What if I lose control?' 'What if she doesn't like me?' 'What if the plane crashes?') which usually ends in some imagined catastrophe (e.g. 'I'll lose control of myself in public and people will laugh at me. I'll never recover from the humiliation of it'). 'What if . . .?' anxious thinking can be transformed into 'Then what . . .?' problem-solving thinking (Padesky and Greenberger, 1995). For example:

What if I can't answer the question?	Then admit that I can't. Ask the audience if someone can or say I will find out the answer.
What if they think I'm stupid?	Then I am probably jumping to conclusions as usual; even if some of them do think that, I don't have to agree with them!
What if I do agree that I'm stupid?	Then I am being very harsh on myself. Being unable to answer a question is simply that. I don't have to turn it into a stick to beat myself with. Learn to focus on improving my performance, not putting myself down.
What if I can't learn to do that?	Then that would be unfortunate, but it is highly likely I will be able to learn it if I put it into daily practice so it becomes a lifelong habit.

Another challenge to 'What if . . .?' negative thinking is to ask 'What if . . .?' positive questions (e.g. 'What if I keep control of myself'; 'What if she does like me?'; 'What if the plane does not crash?'). When you are anxious you rarely if ever give equal time to the positive, literally *opposite* question, 'What if I succeed?' Therein lies a fundamental cognitive bias, because an objective assessment of future outcomes requires the careful consideration of both the positive and negative possibilities. (Newman, 2000: 140; italics in original)

The obvious way to deal with anxiety is to face your fears. This can involve working through a hierarchy of fears (i.e. from least to most frightening) or confronting your worst fear straightaway (this procedure is known as flooding). Whichever path you take, it is important to remain in the feared situation until your anxiety has subsided and cognitive restructuring has occurred, i.e. your thinking has changed, e.g. 'It used to be absolutely awful being in the same room as a spider but now it's just unpleasant'. We would agree with others (e.g. Barlow and Craske 1989; Ellis, 1994) who suggest that it is our statements that create our anxiety such as 'I can't stand it', 'It's terrible', 'It would be awful if that happened'. What does it mean when you say 'I can't stand it' or 'It's terrible'? Your imminent death or the end of the world? The 'it' usually refers to the considerable discomfort you will experience when tackling your fears instead of avoiding them. You can choose to 'stand it' and redefine terrible as 'unpleasant' or 'uncomfortable' as part of your decatastrophizing outlook.

Finally, do not wait until you feel comfortable or confident before you tackle your fears otherwise you will probably be waiting a long time. You can deal with your anxiety while feeling anxious. Doing what you are afraid of eventually extinguishes the fear and allows you to embark on a more exciting and fulfilling life.

Depression

This emotion involves the theme of loss (e.g. of a partner, job, self-esteem, religious faith, sexual potency). Self-devaluation frequently follows a loss (e.g. 'Because I'm impotent, I'm no longer a real man'). When people are depressed they usually withdraw from activities that were previously enjoyable and into themselves, thus reinforcing their depressive state. The negative content of a depressed person's thinking has been called the cognitive triad of depression (Beck *et al.*, 1979): you have a negative view of yourself (e.g. 'I'm no good'), the world (e.g. 'Everything is against me') and your future (e.g. 'I'll never get over this depression'). Accompanying this bleak outlook are, *inter alia*, loss of pleasure, interest, libido, appetite and motivation, poor sleep pattern, rumination, indecisiveness, and suicidal thoughts. Hauck (1974) identifies three causes of depression:

1.   Self-blame: continually criticizing or despising yourself for your failures and setbacks in life (e.g. 'My marriage failed. I can't do anything right. I'm totally useless'). Hauck points out that 'it makes practically no difference what you blame yourself for, just so long as you give yourself hell for it' (1974: 8–9). If you keep on blaming yourself, how will that help you to correct your faults and improve your behaviour?

2.   Self-pity: feeling sorry for yourself over the misfortunes in your life (e.g. 'I didn't deserve to lose my job. Why me? What's the world got against me?'). Life is often arbitrary and unfair but you forget this point when you believe that you deserve to be treated differently, that you have been marked out as a 'special case'.

3.   Other-pity: feeling sorry for the woes of others (e.g. 'It's terrible that famine kills so many children'). Getting depressed over the misfortunes of others does nothing to help them in a practical sense, so what useful purpose does your depression serve? Does your pain lessen the suffering of others?

Negative, distorted thinking is characteristic of depression but, you might argue, surely there are some events, like the death of a partner, that justify being depressed; therefore, in these circumstances, one's thinking is neither distorted nor negative? Having lost a loved partner is distressing but the distortions might creep into your thinking because, for example, you believe 'I'll never be happy again', 'I'll never get over it' or 'Now that he's gone, I'll never have such a perfect love again'. You are predicting your future based on how you are feeling at the present time, but you cannot accurately know how your future will turn out (that can only be determined by looking back, not forward). You can choose to find another partner even if the love you find is less than 'perfect'. Burns distinguishes between sadness and depression:

> Sadness is a normal emotion created by realistic perceptions that describe a negative event involving loss in an undistorted

way. Depression is an illness that *always* results from thoughts that are distorted in some way. (1981: 207; italics in original)

Lazarus (1999) suggests that the mood in sadness is not despairing because you have accepted that the loss (e.g. death of a partner) is irrevocable, i.e. it cannot be restored. Once accepted, you are able to get on with your life. Depression is also tackled by developing a daily activity schedule to keep you busy – action forces you to interrupt your depression-inducing thinking (Dryden and Gordon, 1990). You probably will not feel motivated to undertake much activity so you conclude that you might as well not bother. In fact, motivation comes *after* action: once you force yourself into doing something then the motivation comes to sustain the action. Regular activity will help to improve your energy and mood levels. Thinking and acting against your depressive thoughts and beliefs helps you to overcome your feelings of helplessness ('There's nothing I can do') and hopelessness ('What's the point?') in order to begin to enjoy life again.

Anger

The central theme in anger is some form of perceived transgression against yourself. This can occur in three main areas. Firstly, when you are blocked or thwarted in some way from achieving an important goal (e.g. 'Why the hell didn't those bastards give me the promotion. They know how hard I've worked to get that job'). Secondly, that important personal rules have been violated (e.g. 'When I say "Good morning" to you, I expect the same courtesy from you – you ignorant git!'). Of course, you can be angry at yourself for breaking your own rules (e.g. 'I wasn't supposed to start smoking again. Why the hell can't I keep to what I say?'). Thirdly, when your self-esteem seems threatened in some way (e.g. you verbally insult your friend by calling him a 'scrooge' when he asks you for the return of his loan; in so doing, he has reminded you, intentionally or not, that you failed to have the money ready on the day you said you would).

When you are feeling angry you may verbally or physically lash out (retaliate) or, if deemed not to be an appropriate response in certain circumstances (e.g. to your boss), displace your aggression onto someone or something else (e.g. shouting at your partner or smashing crockery). Instead of attacking, you may withdraw from a situation as when you 'storm out' of a meeting or relationship. You may be reluctant to get even with someone directly (e.g. deriding your ex-partner's sexual inadequacy in front of his new girlfriend) but, instead, do it indirectly (e.g. sending letters to his new girlfriend saying he is a closet homosexual). When this retaliation is expressed indirectly, it is known as passive-aggressiveness. Studies have demonstrated that prolonged anger and hostility increases the risk of coronary heart disease and other physical disorders (Booth-Kewley and Friedman, 1987; Chesney and Rosenman, 1985).

You may believe that letting your anger out is the best way to deal with it and afterwards you will feel purged by your outburst (keeping it in will wreak internal havoc). In our experience, these cathartic expressions of anger only reinforce your anger because the beliefs underpinning it are strengthened rather than weakened (e.g. you rant and rave about your partner leaving you but his 'treachery' lives on corrosively in your mind; you give a colleague a 'piece of my mind' and he replies in kind, exacerbating an already tense situation). As Leahy observes: 'Few people become less angry by becoming more angry' (1996: 44). You may feel that other people should change instead of yourself because they are the 'cause' of your anger. However, you will remain stuck with your anger as it is highly unlikely that others will follow your wishes.

The most effective way for dealing with your anger is stated by Hauck: 'To get over being angry you must first get over the idea you have been taught all your life, namely, that *other people make you angry*' (1980: 37; italics in original; Ellis, 1977). When you are faced with frustrating circumstances or people behaving badly, you have choices about how you wish to respond; if you 'blow your top' rather than feel annoyed or irritated, it is because you have pressed your anger button (e.g. 'I shouldn't be stuck in a bloody traffic jam when I've got to get to an important meeting!'). You may regret your behaviour later which shows that other options were available to you in that situation.

To reinforce our point, imagine waiting in a hospital outpatients' clinic for your appointment which is at 2 p.m. but it is now 3.30 p.m. What would you say to yourself to feel: (a) irritated (e.g. 'I wish they would get a move on'); (b) very angry (e.g. 'What the fucking hell are they doing keeping me hanging around like this. I haven't got all bloody day. Inefficient, useless bastards!'); and (c) irritated again (e.g. 'It's a pain in the neck having to wait this long but I realise they have a lot of patients to see')? This exercise can help you to establish the cause-and-effect relationship between your thoughts and feelings (Gullo, 1993). Your self-talk determines the way you respond to a situation; therefore, any angry outburst is the result of your thinking about the situation, not the situation itself.

We are certainly not arguing that anger is wrong but, instead, would urge you to examine the likely consequences of prolonged anger (e.g. deterioration in physical and psychological health, relationships, work performance, social life) and consider what alternative reactions you would like to adopt. These reactions could include: being more assertive, i.e. standing up for yourself unangrily (see Chapter 7); developing an early warning system by recognizing the signs of incipient anger (e.g. muscle tension, clenched fists, becoming impatient); and learning how to defuse it before it 'explodes' by talking yourself down or leaving the situation until you feel calmer. Once you have calmed down, then you can decide how to deal with the frustration in a more constructive way.

Shame

Shame stems from your assumption that you have revealed publicly a defect, weakness, inadequacy, etc. and that others will agree with your negative self-evaluation. For example, a person who prides himself on his emotional control flies into a rage when stuck in a long supermarket queue; other shoppers turn, stare at him and mutter among themselves. He imagines they think he is bad-tempered and impatient and therefore disapprove of him. As Lazarus points out: 'Shame is a discrepancy between what the person wants to be and the way that person is identified socially' (1999: 239; Kaufman, 1996).

When you feel ashamed, you want to remove yourself from the gaze of others or greatly wish the 'ground to open up and swallow me'. If you cannot withdraw from the situation, you may avoid eye contact or keep your head bowed to avoid what you perceive will be the harsh scrutiny of others. However, feeling trapped in the situation may increase your level of agitation and draw further attention to yourself. Once free of the situation, you may try to avoid going there again as you assume people will never forget your behaviour and point and stare at you when you return.

Sometimes you may feel embarrassed rather than ashamed. Embarrassment can be viewed as a much milder form of shame where weaknesses or flaws you reveal to others are not central to your social identity (e.g. calling someone by the wrong name even though you have met him several times; in my (MN) case, giving a lecture to students who listened politely and then informed me I was in the wrong classroom). When embarrassed, you are able to poke fun at yourself (e.g. 'I'm sorry I got your name wrong. I'm always doing it. I've got a head like a sieve. I'd forget my own name if it wasn't for my wife reminding me of it'), whereas in shame the character failure is usually too painful for any humour to be used.

So far we have focused on external shame (i.e. revealing your imperfections to others and being judged negatively for them); you can also experience internal shame whereby you denigrate yourself for falling below 'some internalised ideal or standard' (Gilbert, 1998: 242). For example, when alone you drink heavily to cope with work-related stress and condemn yourself as weak for not being able to take 'stress in my stride like my colleagues'. You would also probably feel anxious about revealing your 'shameful secret' to others or them finding out about it as you assume they would also condemn you for your 'weakness'.

To start tackling your shame, learn to separate your behaviour from yourself, e.g. 'I may have acted foolishly but that does not make me a fool'; 'I'm drinking to cope with my stress which is not really helping me but that does not make me a weak person' (see section on labelling). If these actions do not make you a 'fool' or 'weak', what do they make you? We would argue that these actions are part of your fallibility and complexity as a human being and therefore you cannot attach a label to yourself which will ever reflect your total or true self (e.g. if you are 'weak', then the only actions you can ever perform are weak ones; does that reflect reality?). If you stop putting yourself down on the basis of your actions, then you can also stop agreeing with others' actual or imagined negative evaluations of you (e.g. 'You might see me as incompetent but I see myself as acting incompetently in certain situations which I'm trying to put right. I don't see myself as an incompetent person. So I'm not going to run away and hide because you see me that way'); in addition, you might try to determine whether people do view you negatively instead of naturally assuming that they do.

An excellent way to change your shame-producing ideas is through shame-attacking exercises (Dryden, 1997; Ellis and MacLaren, 1998). These exercises involve engaging in tasks that will invite public ridicule or criticism (e.g. asking directions to the local railway station while standing outside of it; taking an imaginary dog for a walk) while at the same time accepting yourself for your behaviour (e.g. 'I may act stupidly and people laugh at me because of it, but that doesn't make me a stupid person'). Ensure that your chosen exercises do not involve breaking the law or putting yourself or others in danger. You will need to tolerate the intense anxiety you will probably feel in carrying out these exercises as well as providing yourself with some forceful coping statements to remain in the situation (e.g. 'Put the shame to flight, not myself'). Also, you can learn that nothing terrible will happen to you if people laugh at or disapprove of you: it is the meaning you attach to the laughter or disapproval (e.g. 'I've shown myself to be a complete idiot') rather than the laughter or disapproval itself which leads to your shameful feelings.

These exercises can act as a rehearsal before you carry them out in areas of your life where you wish to make changes (e.g. speaking up in meetings or groups where previously you would have kept quiet for fear of saying something stupid; revealing things about yourself to friends or colleagues such as 'I used to be an alcoholic' because you are no longer afraid of rejection or 'hostile opinion'). These exercises and the philosophy underpinning them can help to free you from the inhibitions of shame and the restrictions they place on your life.

Guilt

The theme in guilt is of a moral violation or lapse. You can feel guilty about actions that primarily affect yourself (e.g. not keeping to your diet, having 'dirty' thoughts) or about the consequences of your actions which hurt or harm others. Your actions that affect others are usually divided into acts of commission (i.e. what you have done), e.g. 'My wife was devastated when she found out about my affair with her sister') and acts of omission (i.e. what you have failed to do), e.g. 'My mate was desperate to talk to someone about his worries but I couldn't be bothered to listen. Now he's in hospital after taking an overdose'). This division is also true for your actions not relevant to others, e.g. 'I ate pork' (act of commission by an orthodox Jew) and 'I didn't pray today' (act of omission by a Muslim). Guilt and shame are often seen as interchangeable but they have similarities as well as differences. As Wessler and Wessler explain:

> [Guilt and shame] result from the same type of ideation and, as far as we can tell, produce the same type of arousal. Both involve doing something considered bad, stupid, or wrong. The difference is the locus of evaluation – external for shame, internal for guilt. Shame comes from receiving the disapproval of others; guilt, from receiving one's own disapproval. In both cases, the conclusion is 'I'm no good'. (1980: 96)

When feeling guilty you may try to 'right the wrong' by, for example, begging forgiveness from the person you believe you have wronged or showering them with presents or affection; you may believe you deserve some form of punishment and administer it yourself (e.g. overdose) or leave it to others (e.g. being beaten up); you may attempt to anaesthetize yourself from the pain of guilt (e.g. drink or drugs or excessive overwork); you may forbid yourself any pleasure until you have expiated your 'sins' (Dryden, 1994a). Behavioural patterns in guilt contrast with those in shame which involve 'concealing, hiding, covering up and running away' (Gilbert, 2000: 175).

A key technique for tackling guilt is to assess your degree of responsibility for an event which you feel guilty about (you may assume you are totally responsible for it). List all the people and factors relevant to the event and give each one a percentage rating (the total must not go above 100 per cent and put yourself last on the list). In the following example, Joan believed she was completely responsible for upsetting her husband when she forgot to buy him a birthday present. This was Joan's redistribution of responsibility:

1 'My husband believes that as I forgot his birthday this means I don't love him any more. This is totally untrue. Those are his ideas, not mine, so that explains why he reacted that way.' 60%
2 'It was extremely busy time at work and, unfortunately, his birthday slipped my mind.' 20%
3 'I could have made a note in my diary to get a birthday present.' 20%

Redistributing responsibility (also known as reattribution) for events is not meant to get you 'off the hook' if you are primarily or totally responsible for an event (e.g. knocking down a pedestrian through drunk driving) but to help you stand back from the event and apportion commensurate responsibility (with Joan's example, she no longer felt guilty, but regretted her oversight in forgetting her husband's birthday and apologized to him for it).

Damning yourself as 'bad' or 'wicked' for violating your moral code may actually encourage you to continue to act in such ways as you neglect to try and understand why you behaved in that way in the first place; in other words, you act in accordance with your self-definition. A more constructive solution is to label your behaviour as 'wrong' or 'bad' (and explore the reasons for it and learn from your errors) but refrain from self-condemnation through self-forgiveness, e.g. 'I know I behaved very badly at the time and I unreservedly apologize for it.' This is more likely to lead to a feeling of remorse for your actions but without guilt because you have avoided self-labelling. If other people are involved, you can explain to them 'why I did what I did', ask for forgiveness but not beg for it, engage in acts of reparation if appropriate (e.g. a financial settlement).

You can also examine the 'should' statements in your moral standards: are they tyrannical (e.g. 'I [absolutely] should never have a moral lapse but if I do this means I'm a bad person') or tolerant (e.g. 'I [preferably] should never have a moral lapse but if I do, this means I'm a fallible human being who regrets his behaviour, not a damnable one')? Tyrannical 'shoulds' are guilt-creating while tolerant 'shoulds' are more likely to generate remorse.

Hurt

When you feel hurt you are reacting to a perceived injustice perpetrated against you (e.g. 'It's not fair that you always put yourself first instead of thinking of my needs sometimes'). You may assume that you have been let down or betrayed by another and conclude that you are undeserving of such treatment. Hurt can be blended with other emotions: self-pitying hurt – e.g. 'I only ever wanted you to love me. I didn't do anything wrong. Why are you treating me like this?'; depressed hurt – e.g. 'I must be worthless because you are treating me like this'; angry hurt – e.g. 'You're a bastard for ignoring my feelings'.

When you are feeling hurt, you will often withdraw from the person who has 'hurt' you and shut down verbal communication with him (this resentful silence or aloofness from others is often referred to as sulking; see Dryden, 1992)). You can engage in silent sulking or angry sulking (e.g. slamming doors around the house) or you may snipe at your partner from time to time without revealing to him what you are hurt about (if he really loves you, then you assume he should know what he has done to upset you). With this behaviour, you hope to get even with or punish your partner in some way (e.g. you attempt to induce guilt in him for his 'selfish' behaviour and then he will ask you for your forgiveness) while avoiding a head-on confrontation. Lazarus suggests that sulking indicates a

> dependence on the other person's attentions and good will. The sulker does not dare make a strong attack lest the other person become totally alienated and the relationship endangered or lost. Sulking presents a picture of neediness, inadequacy, and even childishness. (1999: 227)

In order to overcome hurt, it is important to try and establish the facts of the situation (e.g. 'My wife has gone to bed early. I'll ask her if she is alright') rather than rely on your interpretations of it (e.g. 'She's gone to bed early because she's fed up with me. What did I do wrong?'). Even if you are being treated in an unfair or uncaring way there is no law of the universe or of parliament (except the law in your head) which states that you *must* not be treated in this manner or you *must* get what you believe you deserve (e.g. to be appreciated at all times). Accepting this realistic attitude is more likely to lead to feeling disappointed in your partner's behaviour rather than hurt by it and, instead of sulking, assertively communicating to him what changes you would like to see in his behaviour (e.g. 'I would greatly appreciate it if you would spend a few minutes talking to me when you come home from work instead of going directly to your post and newspapers first'). Time spent sulking could be more usefully employed in seeking improvements in your relationship.

Jealousy

The theme in romantic jealousy is of an actual or imagined threat to your relationship with your partner posed by another (the rival).

Morbid jealousy has been described 'as an excessive irrational pre-occupation with the partner's fidelity for which there is no objective foundation' (Bishay *et al.*, 1996: 9). If you suffer from morbid jealousy, you may infer the following: that your partner's 'desertion' is imminent; that threats exist to your relationship where none actually do; that conversations your partner is having with other men are evidence of her infidelity; that you no longer have the exclusive attention or love of your partner; and that your partner is acting in a way that violates your 'property' rights. Your jealousy is often combined with other emotions: e.g. 'What if she leaves me? I can't survive without her' (anxiety); 'If she is attracted to someone else, then that proves I'm repulsive' (depression); 'I'll smash that bastard's head in for trying to take her away from me' (anger). Hauck (1982a) suggests that it is not the distrust of your partner that causes your jealousy but distrust of yourself: your perceived inability to cope with and see off actual or potential rivals because you are inferior to them (e.g. not attractive or good in bed).

When you are morbidly jealous, you are likely to, *inter alia*, seek constant reassurance from your partner (e.g. 'Do you really love me?'), monitor your partner's behaviour (e.g. 'Did you say you went to the pub on Friday night because Joe said he never saw you there?'), check for signs of infidelity (e.g. checking car seats for any tell-tale 'stains'), restrict your partner's movements (e.g. 'I don't want you to go to that party on Saturday'), and continually accuse your partner of unfaithfulness (e.g. 'Don't lie to me – I know you're seeing him!'). The predictable result of such behaviour is to drive away the very person whom you profess to love so much – your partner!

In mild or moderate jealousy (or what Ellis [1996] calls 'healthy amative heartburn'), you still infer that a threat exists to your relationship with your partner but use this threat as a stimulus to discover what may be going wrong in the relationship and seek to address it constructively (e.g. your partner is fed up with your long working hours and lack of sex and you agree to spend more time with her both in and out of bed). You do not demand the exclusive attention or love of your partner because you realise that he can be attractive to other women (you may even feel proud that you are going out with someone who is so attractive to others!) and attracted to other women without ending up in bed with them.

If infidelity has occurred and you still want to save the relationship, then you can assertively state what new behaviours you expect from your partner and what the consequences will be if he 'relapses'. If, in the final analysis, you are rejected by your partner, you do not have to reject yourself on the basis of his rejection because your self-evaluation is in your hands, not his (e.g. 'He may no longer fancy me but I can still pull if I choose to'). You 'choose to' because relationships are enjoyable and not because your worth as a person depends on being loved. In this way, the ideas that stir morbid jealousy are not transferred to your next relationship.

Envy

When you are envious you desire (covet) the good fortune or advantages possessed by another. Lazarus (1999) suggests that envy can be distinguished from jealousy as the former involves two people (e.g. 'Why does my brother get all the attractive women? I'm just as good looking as he is') whereas jealousy involves three people (e.g. 'Why is that bloke chatting to my wife. Is he trying to seduce her or something?'). We distinguish between resentful and non-resentful envy.

In resentful envy (which may become malicious at times), you will often compare yourself unfavourably with the person who has what you want (e.g. 'I try as hard as she does but she seems to have all the luck while I'm jinxed in some way'); you may denigrate in your mind the value of the desired possession (e.g. 'Admittedly, she's gorgeous but who wants to go out with an airhead? He can have her'); you may convince yourself that you are actually better off without the desired possession and even superior in some way (e.g. 'Winning all that money is going to bring him nothing but grief. I don't envy him at all. In fact, I think you lead a more honest and balanced life without all that money being showered on you'); you may convince yourself that what you have is just the same as or better than what the other person has (e.g. 'Mine might be an older car but it will outlast that flashy pile of junk he's just bought'); you may convince yourself that you will get for yourself what the other person has whether or not you need it; and you may ponder on how to deprive the other person of the object of your desire (e.g. 'That would wipe the smile off his face if I hid or destroyed his lottery ticket so he couldn't collect his winnings').

Your envious thoughts may lead you to act on them by telling the other person what you think of him or his possessions/advantages, by trying to take away the desired possession or by destroying or spoiling it in some way. Gilbert (1989) remarks that envy is rife in competitive cultures where individualism, possessions and success are emphasized. Admitting envy may lead you to feel ashamed because others may see you as mean-spirited or a 'loser'; therefore, you will usually deny that you feel envious.

When you feel non-resentful envy, you will honestly and often openly express your desire for what the other person has but without denigrating her or the desired possession; you may ask her for advice on how to get for yourself what she has (e.g. 'I've always admired your success with men. Any tips on how I can improve my success rate?'); you may genuinely express your support to her for obtaining what you wanted (e.g. 'You got the promotion. Well done') or genuinely commiserate with her misfortunes instead of gloating over them (e.g. 'I'm sorry your business failed. It takes a lot of guts to strike out on your own').

Try not to convince yourself that you are happy with what you have when, in fact, you want to emulate her success (e.g. 'I would like to write a book too'), or not having what she has somehow makes you superior. If you want the desired possession, then ensure it is for your own pleasure and not to prove 'what you can get, so can I'. With this new outlook, you no longer want to deprive her, in thought or deed, of her possessions because you 'allow' her in your mind to have them. You realise that depriving her of them only brings you short-term satisfaction when you see her suffer, but reminds you in the longer-term of your own feelings of resentment and inferiority.

While another person may have the qualities, circumstances, possessions, etc. that you desire, trying to improve your own position in life is more constructive than attempting to destroy or undermine hers.

CONCLUSION

When you encounter emotional difficulties, remember the dictum: you feel as you think. Tap into your internal self-talk and, as we have shown, identify, challenge and change those aspects of your thinking that perpetuate these difficulties. Remember that challenging and changing ingrained ideas requires both thinking and acting differently; if you continue to think and act in the same way, then no change will occur. Maintaining change means continually putting into practice your new ideas and behaviours and monitoring yourself for signs of 'slipping back' (which usually means the resurfacing of old self- and goal-defeating ideas). In other words, you will need to become your own lifelong coach if you want to deal successfully with your troublesome emotions.

Chapter 2

Problem-creating vs problem-solving

INTRODUCTION

What is a problem? This can be defined as 'a present state of facing a particular difficulty without having found an effective solution'. Problems can be of a practical nature (e.g. difficulties with fractious colleagues) or of an emotional nature (e.g. guilt about being off work with illness), though, in practice, these two elements, the practical and emotional, frequently overlap. For example, a person who is depressed (emotional problem) about losing his job (practical problem) sees himself as a failure; this self-image is reinforced by his reluctance to look for another job. He gradually withdraws from others and takes solace in heavy alcohol use. This example can be seen as one of problem-creation, i.e. the person's initial difficulties are added to by the adoption of a counterproductive strategy (though the person's internal experience might suggest it is the right response to make in the circumstances).

In the stress management/problem-solving literature, two important forms of coping have been described: problem-focused coping and emotion-focused coping (Lazarus, 1981; Lazarus and Folkman, 1984; Lazarus, 1999). Problem-focused coping tackles stressful situations in order to change or modify them while emotion-focused coping addresses the emotional distress associated with these situations. If a situation is viewed as unchangeable, then emotion-focused coping is the most realistic strategy to pursue; this is achieved by helping the individual to alter the meaning he attaches to a situation (in the above example, the person decides that losing his job is part of the 'short-term contract culture' rather than as a result of personal deficiencies). Gilbert (2000) observes that problem-solving therapies or techniques are often used with people who are depressed. If problem-creating is replaced by successful problem-solving this will lead to fewer difficulties experienced both internally and externally (D'Zurilla, 1990; D'Zurilla and Nezu, 2000; Ellis, 1994; Grieger and Boyd, 1980; Meichenbaum, 1985; Spivack *et al.*, 1976; Wasik, 1984).

Problem-solving approaches are usually two-pronged because, as Walen *et al.* observe:

Dealing with the emotional problem is necessary, but *not necessarily sufficient:* resolving emotional problems gets rid of emotional disturbance; dealing with *practical* problems leads to self-actualization and improvement in the person's quality of life. Both are important. (1992: 52; italics in original)

While individuals may have combinations of emotional and practical problems, in the following coaching examples, we have focused on emotional problem-solving with the first person and practical problem-solving with the second.

PROBLEM-CREATING: PAUL

Paul worked for a large insurance company. His problems started one Monday afternoon when his manager asked him to have a report on her desk by midday on Friday. He immediately became angry when she was out of ear- and eyeshot: 'As if I haven't got enough bloody work to do already!' He was consumed by his anger for the rest of the afternoon and, as a consequence, little of his existing workload was dealt with.

He took his anger home, provoked a row with his wife and was sharp with his children. He had little sleep that night as he was still angry with his boss and felt guilty and ashamed because of his behaviour towards his family. The next day at work he was very tired and still seething with resentment because of the extra work he had been given; also, he was still brooding on his 'despicable' behaviour from last night. He now had to grapple with catching up on yesterday's work and continued to feel anxious because he had not started on the report. Little productive work was accomplished that day; as he said, 'my mind and emotions were all over the place. Am I losing it or something?'

He vowed to make some preliminary notes about the content of the report after the evening meal but, because he was so tired, fell asleep in a chair while watching television. Despite sleeping all night, he said he did not feel refreshed the next morning. He had a busy day ahead of him but was preoccupied with his inability to start the report he had to deliver in a little over twenty-four hours' time. That evening he decided to go for broke and worked through the night to produce the report. At the office the next day he described himself as the 'walking dead' but delivered his report on schedule.

However, that afternoon he had to chair an important inter-departmental meeting and kept stifling yawns as well trying to stop his head nodding and eyes closing. Over the weekend, instead of winding down, Paul was on tenterhooks about the quality of his report ('I expect it's dreadful') and his chairmanship of the meeting ('probably thought I was on drugs or something'). Relief set in on Monday when his manager said the report was satisfactory and the feedback from the meeting was generally positive apart from his obvious tiredness. Even though Paul was more relaxed and could now focus on his work, he was very troubled as to how he had gone 'out of control last week'.

Problem analysis

In reviewing Paul's work record, he was prone to creating problems about problems (i.e. generating additional problems for yourself [PAP] because you have not tackled the primary problem [PP] constructively) and the aforementioned example was just the most spectacular case to date. In trying to demonstrate vividly this process, I (MN) wrote on the whiteboard in my office:

Primary Problem (PP):	angry about having to write a report in addition to his heavy workload
Problems about Problems (PAP):	falling behind with his workload prolonged anger preoccupation with thoughts of losing control guilty and ashamed about his behaviour towards his family

> lack of sleep
> rising anxiety
> working through the night
> chairing meeting in a very tired
> state
> unable to wind down over the
> weekend

Very soon the whiteboard was covered with Paul's succession of problems. Paul's response was: 'I see so clearly now the train of events, but why didn't I just have a quick temper tantrum, then make a start on the report? I had no problems actually writing the report' (if Paul had difficulties with this or other tasks, then learning some practical problem-solving skills could have supplemented emotional problem-solving).

By using the ABC model of emotional disturbance (Dryden and Gordon, 1993a; Ellis and MacLaren, 1998; Ellis *et al.*, 1997; Palmer and Burton, 1996), Paul was able to pinpoint the disturbance-producing thinking that unleashed his disastrous week. I wrote the model on the whiteboard using Paul's answers to my questions:

A   =   activating event – asked to write a report in addition to his present heavy workload

B   =   disturbance-creating beliefs – 'She shouldn't be doing this to me when I've got enough work already. I'm not bloody well doing it! She shouldn't be snowing me under with all this crap! It's not fair'

C   =   emotional and behavioural consequences – anger, increasing agitation and decreasing work productivity

This simple but insightful model states that it is our self- and task-defeating beliefs at B, not unpleasant or stressful events at A, that largely determine our disturbed emotional and behavioural reactions at C; in other words, A contributes to C but does not cause it.

So why did Paul get into such an emotional tangle? By not dealing with the primary problem (some might call it a challenge or issue) when presented with it; namely, making a start on the report. Once he decided to avoid it or defiantly not do it, the problems about problems process started:

PAUL: When you put it up there on the board, it seems so clear now. Writing reports is part of my job – my boss didn't really ask me to do anything out of the ordinary. I suppose she just asked me at the wrong moment and everything spiralled out of control.

MICHAEL: Well, you let it spiral out of control because of that statement (pointing at the board) 'She shouldn't be doing this to me . . .' and what was it she was actually doing to you at that precise moment?

PAUL: She was asking me to do the report but, like a dog with a bone, I wouldn't let go of the idea that she shouldn't be doing what she was doing.

MICHAEL: And as soon as any individual starts to deny the reality of their situation, problems can start and then quickly escalate.

PAUL: That's exactly what happened to me. I just wouldn't let go of my anger – how dare she give me more work! The thing is though, I want to perform well under pressure because I'm looking for promotion. In fact, it's a funny thing: actually doing the report in the end caused me much less hassle than avoiding it.

MICHAEL: Good point. This is frequently the case: a difficult, boring or unpleasant task may take just an hour or two to complete but often individuals will spend hours, days, weeks or even longer avoiding it.

PAUL: It's crazy when I think about it. I thought my boss was doing my head in with the report when all the time it was me.

MICHAEL: Obviously if you thought you had legitimate grievances about the workload then it would be important to talk to your boss about this issue.

PAUL: Absolutely, but without the anger. Otherwise, the problems about problems stuff will start again.

Problem-solving

Bernard states that 'in order for you to think clearly and thus effectively handle stressful situations and solve practical problems, you first have to develop emotional control. **Emotional self-management is a vital key to stress management**' (1993, section III: 1; emphasis in original). This is achieved by modifying or changing the ideas and beliefs that largely create your emotional and behavioural reactions to events. Thus Paul was taught the additional elements of the ABC model: namely, disputing (D) his disturbance-creating beliefs with the use of reality-testing (i.e. are your beliefs consistent with empirical reality or reality as it actually is at any given moment?) and pragmatism (i.e. do your beliefs and behaviours help or hinder you in achieving your goals?). Through successful disputing, you develop a more rational or personally effective (E) philosophy of living accompanied by a level of emotional arousal (i.e. non-disturbed) which is compatible with effective problem-solving. Paul had clung to reality-denying and disturbance-creating 'shoulds' for several days (and in previous work-related cases) which became the target for further exploration.

Horney (1950) spoke of the 'tyranny of the shoulds' (internal pressurizers) which dictate how self, others or the world should be (e.g. 'I should be rewarded and respected for my hard work'). Of course, the word *should* is not itself either problem-creating or problem-solving; this is determined by the philosophy embedded within the word: in Paul's case, shoulds that deny reality ('She shouldn't be doing this to me . . .') and shoulds that acknowledge empirical reality (see next sentence). As Paul wanted to manage the pressures of the workplace more effectively, he learnt to accept empirical reality at any given moment ('It should be happening because it is!') without necessarily having to like or approve of what he had accepted. What aided the development of this new outlook was DiGiuseppe's motivational syllogism (a syllogism is an argument in which a conclusion is deduced from several premises):

> The first premise is: My present anger is dysfunctional [or counterproductive]. The second premise is: There is an alternative script [new ways of thinking, feeling and behaving] that is more functional. The third premise is: I can control which reaction I have to the activating event. The conclusion is: I need to examine ways in which I can change my emotional reaction. (1995: 148)

Also, acceptance of reality does not mean passivity, resignation or indifference but the starting point to change or modify aspects of it. Therefore, when I focused on Paul's anger, I asked not whether it was justified in the circumstances but what were the consequences for him in holding on to his anger (e.g. the tasks took longer to complete). This approach usually yields a more productive outcome than challenging the basis of a person's anger as the

latter strategy can reinforce the 'rightness' of their anger (Terjesen
et al., 1997). By examining the self-defeating, family-disrupting and
task-blocking consequences of his anger, Paul was more likely to
initiate self-change. But if he was to give up his anger, what feeling
was going to take its place?

Paul's plan of action

As Paul wanted to avoid the disastrous chain of events that
unfolded when he got angry about having to write the report, he
left a message on his desk, prominently displayed, which read:
'When it happens, deal with it.' The 'it' could refer to any task,
crisis, setback, etc. By gradually internalizing this new attitude, he
realized he could control his emotional reactions to workplace
events; instead of anger he now experienced what he called a 'get
on with it irritability'. He cited an example of being an eleventh-
hour replacement to chair a meeting:

PAUL: Six months earlier if I'd been asked I would have got myself
into a right old angry state, you know saying things like 'I
shouldn't be put in this position' and 'They should have given
me adequate warning' and so on.

MICHAEL: And now . . .?

PAUL: Well, I wasn't exactly overjoyed at the prospect but I
immediately swung into action by quickly reviewing the background information to the key agenda items. This info came
off the fax and I was reading it on the way to the meeting.
Things went pretty smoothly. My manager thanked me for
doing a good job. The secret I've discovered is to get hold of
the problem straightaway and do something about it.

MICHAEL: And what if you can't do something about it straightaway . . .?

PAUL: Well, I'll just put it on hold until I can do something about it
or accept the situation if I can't do anything about it at all. But
whichever way it goes, I no longer get stressed-out about it . . .
most of the time. Rome wasn't built in a day you know.

MICHAEL: And if you did get really stressed-out, would you say at
that point something like 'I shouldn't get stressed out now as
I've learnt to handle things differently'?

PAUL: (*laughs*) No, I would say 'I am stressed-out' which would
acknowledge the reality of how I feel and then that would act

as a self-administered kick up the backside to get myself back under control. It would be nice not to get stressed-out or angry in the first place.

MICHAEL: Unlikely though. Remember, emotional self-management does not mean you will never get distressed again but that you can greatly reduce the frequency, intensity and duration of such distress.

PAUL: I'll settle for that.

PROBLEM-CREATING: DIANA

Diana had changed careers in order to train as a stress management counsellor. Since her training ended, she had not applied to any local companies for work. She wanted to feel 'really confident' before undertaking any stress management work and 'ensure that I made the right career change by not failing'. She knew that gaining confidence and becoming successful were more likely to occur *after* a period of effort, not before it; however, as these outcomes could not be guaranteed, she felt stymied by her need for certainty. She decided that some further training 'might do the trick' but the hoped for confidence did not materialize. She could not really afford the courses as the 'money was going out but nothing coming in'.

Diana saw her new career slipping away before it even got started; she was becoming paralysed by inaction. She even thought of trying to get her old job back: 'I suppose I could slink back as a failure'. What compounded her disappointment in herself was seeing some of her colleagues on the original course now getting some industrial work: 'Why them and not me?' She considered herself a poor role model as a stress management counsellor because she was not handling her present problems in a constructive and realistic way: 'How can I teach stress management to others when I can't seem to solve my own problems.' She knew that 'make or break' time was not far away as financial pressures were mounting.

Problem analysis

Diana's difficulties were viewed within the framework of a seven-step problem-solving model (Wasik, 1984):

Steps	Questions/Actions
1. Problem identification	What is the concern?
2. Goal selection	What do I want?
3. Generation of alternatives	What can I do?
4. Consideration of consequences	What might happen?
5. Decision making	What is my decision?
6. Implementation	Now do it!
7. Evaluation	Did it work?

Step 1: Problem identification

Diana described her problem as having 'no confidence in myself as a stress management counsellor'. Butler and Hope (1996) suggest reformulating problems in terms that suggest they can be solved rather than remain unsolvable:

MICHAEL: Have you had confidence in yourself before?

DIANA: Of course, and I can give you plenty of examples, but it seems to have deserted me in this instance. I really want to succeed so much because I've burnt my bridges in changing careers.

MICHAEL: But is it success you're worried about?

DIANA: No, it's failing. That's what is holding me back.

MICHAEL: How can you state your problem in terms which imply that progress can be made?

DIANA: Well, something like how to develop confidence in myself as a stress management counsellor.

MICHAEL: What about the failure part?

DIANA: I suppose see setbacks and failures as part of the learning experience.

MICHAEL: And what has your learning experience taught you so far?

DIANA: If I don't make a start soon, I will definitely fail in my new career.

During step 1, your strengths, abilities and problem-solving skills can be noted down in order to determine whether you will be able to use the problem-solving model at the present time (if you are too emotionally distressed you can use the ABCDE model to combat and change your disturbance-producing thinking before you focus on the seven-step model). If you have trouble identifying your problem, it may be useful to state your goals and then work backwards to pinpoint what is stopping you from achieving them.

Step 2: Goal selection

Goals need to be stated in specific and behavioural terms that allow for measurement of your progress, e.g. 'I want to make three job applications per week over the next month'. Vague or unrealistic goals should be avoided, e.g. 'I want things to be better' and 'Other people must think well of me'. Goals should also be within your area of control rather than outside of it, e.g. 'I want my colleague to take on more of the work rather than dump it on me all the time' means that the responsibility for achieving the goal rests with the 'work avoidance' colleague who is hardly likely to comply! The person's goal, within her control, might be: 'I want to learn to be assertive so I can challenge her about this issue and hopefully bring about some changes in the distribution of workloads.' Diana defined her goal as 'getting work as a stress management counsellor':

MICHAEL: Who actually gives you the work?
DIANA: The employer, the company.
MICHAEL: So is that within your control?
DIANA: No.
MICHAEL: What is within your control?
DIANA: Letting people, companies know that I exist. Pushing myself forward. That can be the start of gaining confidence. Doing rather than stewing.
MICHAEL: So how many contacts do you hope to make per week, per month?
DIANA: I want to aim for six contacts per week over the first month.

Step 3: Generation of alternatives

This step involves you generating as many solutions as possible to reach your goals no matter how ludicrous some of them initially appear; in other words, to brainstorm or let your imagination rip (evaluation of their potential usefulness comes at the next step). If you find it difficult to get started on this process, ask a friend to suggest some solutions for you. If this block occurs in our coaching sessions, we may suggest to our clients some wild or extreme ideas to nudge their thinking along, e.g. 'Ask a hundred women out in the next week'. Clients' usual responses to such ideas are to suggest more moderate ones (e.g. 'Maybe one or two rather than a hundred'). Diana's solutions were:

(a) 'Blitz every company in the country with my CV and brochure.'
(b) 'Only concentrate on local companies and follow up my stuff with a phone call to introduce myself.'
(c) 'Talk to my colleagues and find out how they got their foot in the door.'
(d) 'Offer my services to local voluntary groups and organizations like the Women's Institute and the Rotary Club.'
(e) 'Send my stuff to local health authorities, education and social services departments, GP surgeries, gyms.'
(f) 'Put a leaflet through everybody's door in my neighbourhood.'

Step 4: Consideration of consequences

This involves you considering the advantages and disadvantages of each solution produced from the brainstorming session and the likely consequences of implementing each solution. You may wish to rate the usefulness of each possible solution on a 0–10 scale (0 = least useful to 10 = most useful). Diana considered her solutions thus:

(a) 'I'm not ready for this and the costs would be prohibitive. Ruled out.' 0
(b) 'This seems more realistic but I would be worried about my lack of experience and therefore would I be value for money at this stage?' 4
(c) 'Good idea. I'm bound to get some sound advice.' 6
(d) 'This strikes me as the best way forward at the present time: I'd be getting much-needed practice and feedback, though no money yet, and maybe they won't be as tough an audience as I imagine they might be in business and industry. I'm sure this is the way to break through my lack of confidence barrier.' 8

(e) 'The same reservations as at solution two.' 4

(f) 'Only if I get really desperate.' 1

Step 5: Decision making

You now choose the most feasible or promising solution(s) evaluated in the previous step which appears to have the least disadvantages and seems most likely to achieve your stated goals. Diana chose solutions (c) and (d). This step also involves means–ends thinking, i.e. planning a series of steps in order to execute the chosen solution to achieve your goals (Platt *et al.*, 1986; Dryden *et al.*, 1999). For example, if a person's goal is to stand up for himself in difficult social situations then he might need to learn assertion skills, rehearse these skills before carrying them out in the target situation, anticipate obstacles and plan how to overcome them (if he gets a hostile reception, does he want to revert to his previously passive state in these situations?).

Step 6: Implementation

D'Zurilla (1990) makes the important distinction between problem-solving and solution-implementation: the former refers to discovering solutions to problems while the latter refers to carrying out solutions in actual situations. Therefore 'some individuals may possess good problem-solving skills but poor solution-implementation skills, or vice versa' (D'Zurilla, 1990: 333); it is important to assess both sets of skills for a problem-solving programme. If you have poor solution-implementation skills, some training will be necessary (e.g. time management, communication, relaxation).

Diana went to the library for a list of local voluntary organizations and started contacting them with offers of a stress management presentation; in some cases, she followed this up with a visit. Three groups accepted her offer. However, she was still worried about 'my lack of practice' and suggested a solution to this that had not occurred to her at step 3: could she give a presentation to me (MN) as part of her coaching sessions? I agreed and brought in some of my colleagues to give her a bigger audience. We gave her a balanced appraisal of her presentation; she was both grateful for the evaluation and relieved that 'I've now got one under my belt'. As Hauck emphasizes, this is how self-confidence develops:

You never fail as long as you are trying. Each trial teaches you something *if* you study your behavior. You're getting valuable feedback from each effort, and this information is a small segment of success. Don't knock it. If you repeat the trials often enough, you add up little successes until they become noticeable. The upshot is that you are failing *only* when you are not trying, never otherwise. (1982b: 60; italics in original)

Diana was taught coping imagery (Palmer and Dryden, 1995) whereby she imagined getting mostly negative feedback for a presentation and seeing this as an opportunity for learning and improvement instead of condemning herself. She agreed to carry out this imagery exercise on a daily basis in the run-up to her presentations as part of 'Diana's Development Programme'.

Step 7: Evaluation

This step involves assessing your progress by considering the out-come of your action in relation to your goal. Has your goal been achieved? If not, what obstacles did you find difficult to overcome? Was it the right solution? Did you persist enough or did you give up too quickly? Are there further skills you need to acquire to make goal-attainment more likely? Finding a satisfactory solution to your problems is usually a combination of trial and error and persistence (see Chapter 5 for a discussion of persistence).

Diana said that her three presentations to local voluntary agencies went 'reasonably well' and she felt more confident. She said that the next stage was 'to get my foot in the door of local companies and start making some money'. To that end, she chose solution (b) generated at step 3. 'Picking the brains' of her colleagues had yielded some good ideas that she would use in her 'doorstepping' activities. Diana concluded that 'confidence comes in small steps and struggle rather than the great leap and ease that I wanted'. Diana was learning to become her own problem-solver. Follow-up coaching sessions were agreed with Diana to determine whether she was maintaining her problem-solving gains as well as generalizing the problem-solving model to other areas of her life (i.e. using steps 1–6 again to tackle a new problem).

If your solution has, for whatever reason, proved ineffective you can return to step 5 and pick another solution previously generated at step 3 or generate and choose new ones based on what you have learnt from your experiences (e.g. 'I really do need some professional help with this particular problem'). Once you gain some proficiency at using this seven-step model, you may find it unwieldy or long-winded. If this is the case, you can use the five-step SOLVE model (McKay *et al.*, 1997):

State your problem

Outline your goals

List your alternatives

View the consequences

Evaluate your results

For those of you who want an even shorter model for rapid processing of a problem in order to deal with a crisis or make a quick decision, try PIE (with this model, you may experience a less satisfactory outcome than with the five- or seven-step models because deliberation is exchanged for speed):

Problem definition

Implementation of chosen solution

Evaluation of outcome

CONCLUSION

Problem-creating is easily done. One form discussed in this chapter is reality-denying 'should' statements which frequently lead to emotional disturbance and the generation of additional problems. The antidote to this kind of thinking is suggested by Walen *et al.*:

> Accepting an unfortunate reality and not getting overly upset about it acknowledges that the reality exists, that it is unpleasant, that it would be irrational to demand or insist that it should not have happened, and that we will attempt to change it, if we can [or deal with it more effectively]. (1992: 22)

Our second example of problem-creating focused on a person's lack of confidence about achieving success in her new career; she

wanted to feel confident *before* seeking work yet knew that confidence comes from performance, not in the absence of it. By
following a practical problem-solving model, she was encouraged
to systematically think her way through to identifying, implementing and evaluating some confidence-building activities.

Whether your problems are emotional or practical, or a combination of the two, we hope that these two models of problem-
solving will help you in their resolution.

Chapter 3

Overcoming procrastination

INTRODUCTION

A common dictionary definition of procrastination is 'to defer action', i.e. to decide deliberately to do something later on (e.g. 'I have deferred my decision until next Wednesday'). This is an example of planned delay in order to consider all the available evidence before making the decision. However, when individuals have problems with procrastination it usually refers to them acting in a dilatory manner and thus laying something aside until a future unspecified time (e.g. 'I will do it eventually'); or, if a future time has been specified, no action occurs when the time arrives (e.g. 'I was going to start the essay today but a friend popped round and one thing led to another'). To put the problem of procrastination simply: you keep putting off doing what your better judgement tells you should be done now (incidentally, procrastinate is often confused with prevaricate which means 'to act or speak evasively or misleadingly'). Sometimes procrastination is accompanied by self-condemnation (e.g. 'I want to knuckle down but I'm so bloody useless at doing it').

WHAT HOLDS YOU BACK?

You know what needs to be done yet you cannot get on with it. What blocks you from engaging in productive action? Hauck suggests that poor self-discipline is an unsurprising human trait as 'avoiding a difficult situation seems like the most natural course to take because we are so easily seduced by immediate satisfactions' (1982b: 18). Glucksman believes that 'family styles have a lot to do with it, whether you grow up in a family of procrastinators, so you learn it from your parents and those around you. Certain personality types [e.g. perfectionists] tend to be procrastinators' (1990: 8a). Dryden (1994b) observes that procrastination is often a behavioural way of protecting yourself from experiencing an unpleasant emotional state (e.g. you prefer to watch television instead of starting on your pile of paperwork because if you do make a start on it, you will experience intense irritation). A form of procrastination which might be difficult to detect is the 'comfort of discomfort' paradox: your current miserable or non-productive state is familiar and safe compared with the feared consequences of change and subsequent failure. Therefore, your claim that 'I'm happy the way that I am' is not so much a statement of genuine contentment but a fear of being even worse off if the change process fails. Hence you decide to stay in your rut rather than attempt to leave it.

CAUSES OF PROCRASTINATION

Dryden and Gordon (1993b; Ellis and Knaus, 1977) identify three main causes of procrastination:

1. Anxiety. This is based on perceived threats to your self-esteem if you engage in the avoided task. Some examples: imagine asking someone out for a date instead of avoiding it. The prospect of doing so starts to make you feel anxious because you believe you will be turned down by the person you ask and this will confirm in your mind that you are unattractive. You continually put off writing an article because you fear it will be rejected for publication thereby proving that 'I have no talent'. You loaf around the house all day instead of working on your college essay because if you do start it, you have visions of it not being good enough to achieve a top grade and thereby exposing you as a failure. Avoiding these activities helps to keep your anxiety and the associated feared consequences 'out of sight' in the short-term but perpetuates your problems in the longer-term (e.g. your life remains devoid of romance and sexual activity).

2. Low frustration tolerance (LFT). This refers to your perceived inability to endure frustration, boredom, hard work, uncomfortable feelings, setbacks, etc., so unpleasant tasks are avoided

or quickly given up when started. The philosophical core of LFT is: 'I can't stand present pain for future gain.' For example, you want to become fit but the effort involved in achieving your goal is deemed by you as 'too much' and you resign yourself to staying unfit. A friend of mine (MN) won a holiday for two in Barbados but he was required by the travel company to go London to fill in some forms. He told me he could not be bothered with 'all the hassle' and consequently he lost the holiday. His partner 'hit the roof', told him it was typical of his general attitude and then walked out on him. LFT is a deceptive philosophy because it encourages you to think you are winning by avoiding unpleasant tasks or situations whereas your life actually becomes much harder in the long run as your unresolved problems mount up.

3. Rebellion. This is used as a way of expressing your anger towards others by delaying important tasks – you want to get back at someone for being told what to do or how to behave. For example, your partner keeps on at you to make sure that your tax returns are sent in before the deadline. However, you resent being spoken to 'as if I'm a child' and deliberately miss the deadline 'to show her', but you incur a financial penalty which you dislike having to pay. Your boss tells you to carry out some additional work for him; you bristle with indignation at being treated like 'his bloody slave' and your 'I'll show him' attitude results in poor-quality work and missed deadlines. Your 'bolshie' attitude is noted and leads to you not being considered for promotion. Your desire to get back at others often rebounds unfavourably on you.

Anxiety, LFT and rebellion may all be found in a single instance of procrastination. For example, your boss tells you to get back to her with a date for a workshop she wants you to run on improving workplace performance. You procrastinate over nominating a date because you are angry with her for 'dumping this job on me instead of buying in professionals to do it'. Your procrastination also involves a great distaste for all the preparatory work you will have to do for the workshop as well as your fear that it will be a flop and you will be seen as incompetent.

People who regularly procrastinate often delay in two major areas: self-development and personal maintenance (Knaus, 1993).

Self-development refers to attempts to realise desired goals, e.g. changing one's job or career, seeking new partners, developing an exciting social life. Personal maintenance involves undertaking tasks which make life easier, e.g. doing housework, paying bills on time, answering correspondence, repairing the car. Such delays can increase the frustrations and decrease the pleasures in your life. Wessler and Wessler state that 'almost any behavior can be the object of procrastination' (1980: 104).

PUTTING THINGS OFF

Avoidance behaviours and the rationalizations that accompany them can include the following:

- Contemplating the task at hand without actually engaging in it, e.g. sitting in an armchair for long periods thinking about putting up shelves, 'I need to get the feel of a job before I actually start it'. Armchair contemplation will not help you get the 'feel' of a task, but doing it will.

- You leave tasks until the last minute because 'I do my best work under pressure'. To verify this claim, you would need to compare the quality of your 'last minute' work with your 'starting earlier' work. This might trigger the real problem such as the sheer, boring grind of working longer on the task. Working under pressure means you have 'to rush to complete it, cannot assemble all the relevant materials to help you do it well, have little time to look it over and review it, and often have to polish it off in a relatively unfinished, glossed-over manner' (Ellis and Knaus, 1977: 137).

- When you claim 'I'll do it tomorrow' you may try to convince yourself that you mean it or 'the job is as good as done'. In reality, tomorrow is not the next day but a hazy point in time in the distant future. Like the pub sign which says 'Free beer tomorrow', the promise of action tomorrow is not fulfilled. Action today can mean less worry and more opportunities tomorrow.

- A variation on the 'I'll do it tomorrow' theme is making future action contingent upon present problem-solving, e.g. 'I'll start asking women out when I've lost a bit of weight and have had a few sessions at the gym so I can feel better about myself'. Diverting yourself into these activities, weight loss and getting fitter, which may be undertaken only half-heartedly or not at all, keeps you from facing your real problem – in this instance, fear of rejection and putting yourself down on the basis of it ('Women don't fancy a slob like me').

- Previously unimportant tasks suddenly become all-important thereby pushing the unpleasant task into the background, e.g. 'The house needs a spring-clean. I can't be expected to fill in all this paperwork sitting in a dirty house.' If the unpleasant task was to magically disappear, would the house still need an immediate spring-clean?

- Pleasurable pursuits are undertaken first as a way of encouraging yourself to eventually face the difficult task, but the pleasures linger thereby pushing the task back to another time, e.g. 'Why spoil a good thing? There's plenty of time to cut the grass on another day.' Of course, you can enjoy yourself and cut the grass on the same day.

- You are continually alert to any seemingly plausible reason to resist beginning or desisting from the task, e.g. 'The phone's ringing and it could well be an important call. My husband could be in trouble.' Once the phone call is finished, you may look for other ways to distract yourself from the task (e.g. having a cup of coffee, writing out a shopping list) or tell yourself that you have lost your momentum to continue on it. You could force yourself back into the task and surprise yourself how quickly you can recover your momentum.

- Creating the illusion of tackling the task, i.e. to all intents and purposes you are carrying out work that seems to be a precursor to the task itself, e.g. tidying your desk and the room before settling down to write an essay. However, once the preparatory work is done – 'A tidy room is a tidy mind' – you consider that you have done enough for the time being; actually writing the essay, or at least starting it, is avoided but you convince yourself that you have 'made a start on it' and can now turn your mind to something more pleasurable. Illusions can be comforting but they do not write essays for you.

- Calling yourself 'lazy', 'a slow starter' or 'a hopeless case' allows you to justify your procrastination as well as deflect criticism from others who complain about your tardiness, e.g. 'I can't help being this way'. If you were to stop hiding behind your name-calling and got down to business, you might experience the real problem – not your 'laziness' but your fear of failure for example.

- Waiting to feel motivated before you start a task as you reason with yourself that you can hardly be expected to carry out a difficult task in an unmotivated state or if you are not in the right mood. As Burns points out: 'Motivation doesn't come first – productive action does. You have to prime the pump by getting started whether you feel like it or not. Once you begin to accomplish something, it will often spur you on to do even more' (1989: 170).

- Telling yourself to 'let sleeping dogs lie' even though you feel aggrieved about your partner's selfish behaviour. To confront him about his behaviour might lead to feared consequences (e.g. he leaves you). Therefore, you delay asserting yourself 'until the right moment arrives'. That moment is unlikely to arrive unless you 'wake the dogs up'.

People can also procrastinate over things that could well benefit them rather than have negative consequences. Glucksman suggests that this happens because some people 'are afraid of success or afraid of really feeling pleasure or feel they don't deserve it. And in a sense, it's a form of self-punishment or a form of undermining themselves' (1990: 8a).

TYPOLOGY OF PROCRASTINATION

Sapadin (1997) has offered a typology of chronic procrastination:

1. Perfectionism – you are reluctant to start or finish tasks because you might not achieve your uncompromisingly high standards. Therefore, you may find excuses to explain your less-than-perfect performance in order to avoid self-condemnation, e.g. 'I didn't get a grade A for the exam because I was partying too

much. If I had done some serious studying and got less than an A, then I really would be a failure.'

2. Dreaming – you have a tendency towards vagueness and lack of realism; grandiose ideas are not translated into achievable goals. You use fantasy as an escape from the dreariness or seemingly unchangeable pattern of your life.

3. Worry – you fear things going wrong and being overwhelmed by events; therefore, you avoid risk or change and have little confidence in your ability to make decisions or tolerate discomfort.

4. Crisis making – you like to display bravado in declaring you cannot get motivated until the eleventh hour or this is when you do your best work. Living 'on the edge' gives you an adrenaline rush. You usually exhibit a very low threshold for boredom. Alternatively, in eleventh-hour procrastination, you hope the task will miraculously disappear or someone will appear to help you with it or do it for you.

5. Defiant – (a) you are aggressive and argumentative towards others' suggestions or instructions because they mean you are being told what to do or that other people are trying to control you; or (b) you are passive–aggressive in style and say 'yes' when you mean 'no' as a means of indirectly getting back at someone else because you are openly afraid or reluctant to voice your true feelings.

6. Overdoing things – you are always working at something and often making extra work for yourself, yet you do not focus on the important issues that need to be tackled (e.g. deciding what your real goals and values are in life). You have difficulty saying 'no' and delegating work.

THE COMMON DENOMINATOR OF PROCRASTINATION

According to Dryden and Gordon, the 'one thing all people who procrastinate have in common . . . is a clear-cut emotional problem' (1993b: 59). You may not be aware of your own emotional problem because your avoidance behaviour (also known as safety behaviour) protects you from experiencing it. The way to 'release' this emotion is to face the avoided situation and identify the beliefs and thoughts maintaining the procrastination. The ABC model of emotional problems helps you to understand this process:

A   =   activating event – you imagine asking questions and making comments at a meeting (instead of keeping silent or saying very little which is your usual pattern of behaviour)

B   =   beliefs and thoughts – 'I'll say the wrong thing or get my facts confused and look an idiot in the eyes of others'

C   =   emotional consequences – intense anxiety

By exposing yourself in imagination to what you normally avoid (A) triggers but does not cause your intense anxiety at C. How you feel at C is mediated by your beliefs and thoughts at B; namely, that you will look an idiot in the eyes of others when you give your opinions. By keeping quiet at meetings, your anxiety-provoking thinking is not activated and you remain 'safe'. We will return to the use of this model later in the chapter.

TACKLING PROCRASTINATION

When we ask individuals how they would feel if they got on with the task instead of avoiding it, they often reply 'great'. The next question is why are they depriving themselves of this highly pleasurable feeling by avoiding the task. Anticipating feeling great does not mean that you have suddenly become motivated to carry out the task. There is a discomfort phase to get through which still acts as a deterrent to initiating the task; it is important to explore this discomfort phase in order to discover what holds you back (e.g. it might be a feeling of being overwhelmed by the task and, therefore, you are reluctant to persevere with it in order to start feeling more in control of what you are doing).

The most obvious solution to procrastination might be an action plan (e.g. time management schedule) in order to generate greater personal productivity; however, we would argue against this because, as we have already shown, procrastination is underpinned by emotional problems. You are not usually at your practical problem-solving best when you are emotionally upset (Dryden and

Neenan, 1995) or by 'relieving practical problems before emotional problems tends to rob clients of their motivation to solve their emotional problems, leaving them more comfortable yet still disturbed' (Grieger and Boyd, 1980: 36). Therefore, we usually suggest a two-pronged attack on procrastination: first tackle its emotional aspects before focusing on its practical aspects. The following coaching sessions with David will illustrate these principles in practice.

Assessing the problem

DAVID: I'm missing deadlines at work with some of the projects I've been given to do. I can't seem to get motivated and therefore can't get started on them straightaway. When I eventually get going it's all in an undisciplined rush driven by guilt.

MICHAEL: What are the consequences of missing deadlines?

DAVID: My boss gets pissed off and I keep on apologizing to her with some pathetic excuse. I worry what my colleagues think of me. I feel guilty about not meeting the deadlines. I should be able to cut the mustard like most of my colleagues can.

MICHAEL: Are there any benefits from not getting on with it?

DAVID: Well, if I put these projects on the back burner then I can get on with something that's more enjoyable. It doesn't last long though because I start to worry again about missing the deadlines.

MICHAEL: Could you lose your job over your tardiness?

DAVID: I suppose I could but I assure you I don't want that to happen. I would love to be able to get going on these projects as soon as I'm given them. I want to stop messing about.

MICHAEL: Okay, let's take a closer look at this lack of motivation issue.

People who procrastinate often become emotionally upset about their inability to 'get on with it' or face up to the problem. These emotions (worry and guilt in the above example) are best viewed as secondary rather than as primary because they are a result of the procrastination, not the reason for it. The cognitive–emotive factors (i.e. thoughts and feelings) that maintain procrastination are the main coaching focus. Much time can be wasted on discussing these secondary emotional problems thereby prolonging the person's procrastination in the coaching sessions! A caveat to this point is that you could be so preoccupied by these secondary problems that no productive work can occur on the primary problem until these secondary emotional issues are addressed (Dryden and DiGiuseppe, 1990). David was asked if he would be absorbed or distracted by these secondary problems in our quest to understand what drives his procrastination. He said 'no' and was keen to find an answer to his avoidance behaviour.

I (MN) explained to David that procrastination often acts as a safety behaviour protecting the individual from an unpleasant or feared experience. However, the safety behaviour serves to maintain the underlying problem rather than solve it. Therefore, the 'way in' to understand the process of procrastination is to help the person reveal the irrational (i.e. self- and task-defeating) ideas that maintain the problem. This 'irrationality identification phase is important in that if you do not see how you are stopping yourself, then it will be quite difficult for you to change' (Knaus, 1993, section 2: 35). This phase can be completed through a process known as inference chaining which links the person's personally significant inferences about an event or situation in order to uncover his disturbance-producing thinking through a series of 'Let's assume . . . then what?' questions (Neenan and Dryden, 1999):

MICHAEL: Now close your eyes David and vividly imagine that you are starting on one of these avoided projects in an unmotivated and uninspired state. What specific project can you think of?

DAVID: Collating customer replies to one of our latest products.

MICHAEL: How are feeling as you start the project?

DAVID: Apprehensive, irritable.

MICHAEL: You are feeling that way because . . .?

DAVID: Because it's boring and I have no interest in doing it . . . until I'm reluctantly forced into it by the looming deadline.

MICHAEL: Okay, but you're going to do it now rather than wait and be forced into it. What else is going through your mind?

DAVID: Why should I put myself through this when I don't have to yet?

MICHAEL: Let's assume you are putting yourself through it, then what?

DAVID: (*becoming agitated*) I'm going to get even more angry. I'll probably chuck all the bloody paperwork into the waste bin. I shouldn't have to do things that are boring.

MICHAEL: Let's assume you are going to force yourself to do things that are boring, then what?

DAVID: I'm going to get really fed up, bored stiff, angry, maybe rude to others. So why should I put myself through that experience?

MICHAEL: Okay, open your eyes. There seems to be two issues here: first, that you shouldn't have to do boring tasks when you're unmotivated or uninterested; second, if you do have to do them when you don't want to, you're going to get very upset about it. Would you agree with this analysis?

DAVID: Yes, I'd go along with it.

MICHAEL: Which of these two issues is more important to you: the lack of motivation or getting upset while carrying out these tasks?

DAVID: I don't follow what you mean.

MICHAEL: Well, if you were motivated to carry out these projects would you get upset about doing them?

DAVID: Probably not, but I really can't see myself becoming that motivated about them. These projects are pretty boring.

MICHAEL: Okay, what about if you were able to get on with these boring projects straightaway without being motivated but able to tolerate your anger?

DAVID: Hmm. I like the sound of that. (*laughs*) How do I do it then?

MICHAEL: Well, what's the worst thing that will happen to you if you remain angry while working on one of your projects?

DAVID: Er . . . what's the worst thing? . . . just putting up with it I suppose until it wears off.

MICHAEL: Will it be the end of your world or will you never be happy again if you have to tolerate feeling angry until it wears off?

DAVID: Of course not. It's learning to put up with my anger.

MICHAEL: With a different attitude in mind. How do you learn to put up with your anger?

DAVID: (*laughs*) Getting on with things and putting up with how I feel. So how do I get this new attitude?

David was taught the cognitive-behavioural coaching viewpoint that our beliefs and attitudes about events rather than the events themselves largely create our emotional upsets and counter-productive behaviours. The ABC model of emotional problems was drawn on a whiteboard to show the goal-blocking beliefs that maintained David's procrastination:

A 1 = Undertaking a boring task when unmotivated
B 1 = 'I shouldn't have to do what I don't want to do!'
C 1 = Irritability
A 2 = David notices how irritable he is
B 2 = 'I shouldn't have to feel like this and I can't stand it!'
C 2 = Anger about feeling irritable

Whether David starts the project or avoids it depends on whether the intensely unpleasant feelings at C2 are greater than at C1. As they are, David's behaviour is motivated by the avoidance of feeling angry. However, as the deadline comes ever closer, David's fear of missing it propels him into hasty action. Until that time comes, David avoids the anger associated with undertaking the project. In discussing this model with David, he disclosed that in certain areas of his life (not just at work) he exhibited what we came to pinpoint as low frustration tolerance (LFT): 'If I'm going to feel pretty unpleasant about some task or activity, then I do my best to avoid doing it or put it off as long as possible because I can't stand feeling that way.' The antidote to LFT is to strive for higher frustration tolerance (HFT) by internalizing a coping attitude to emotional upsets, setbacks and discomfort in life (e.g. 'I don't like experiencing these unpleasant feelings but I can learn to tolerate them as it will help me to achieve my goals').

MICHAEL: What kind of attitude do you need to develop if you want to get to grips with this problem?
DAVID: Something like 'Stop moaning about how I feel and get on with it'.
MICHAEL: How will that help you?
DAVID: So I can meet my deadlines, not leave it to the last minute when it all becomes an undisciplined rush, as I've said before.
MICHAEL: So what will be the first step then?
DAVID: Well, I'm not starting a project tomorrow – I'm not that keen yet. Let's take it a little easier to start with.
MICHAEL: Okay, are there any things at home that you avoid for the same reasons?
DAVID: Yes. DIY tasks that my wife keeps on about and some social occasions I put off because they'll bore me.

MICHAEL: How about carrying out a few of these tasks in order to prove to yourself . . .?

DAVID: I won't like doing them because of the way I'm going to feel but that is no reason for me to avoid doing them. Yes, I'll do a few.

The course of coaching

These and other tasks that David agreed to carry out are often called 'stay-in-there' assignments and consist of 'staying in rather than avoiding an aversive situation in order to work through the disturbed ideas and feelings about it' (Grieger and Boyd, 1980: 156). Stay-in-there tasks can be carried out implosively (i.e. immediately and fully) or gradually by desensitizing yourself to less unpleasant situations or tasks before moving on to the most unpleasant ones. David was cognitively prepared to enter these situations with rational coping statements such as 'I don't like it [emotional discomfort] but I can and will put up with it' and thereby learnt to tolerate unpleasant feelings and situations.

Imagery was employed to promote constructive change. The technique used was rational-emotive imagery (REI, Maultsby and Ellis, 1974) whereby David was asked to imagine feeling extremely angry while carrying out a usually avoided task and then, while staying with the same task, to diminish his level of negative affect (emotion) so he now only felt mildly irritable. The affective shift was achieved by cognitive modification: from 'I can't stand feeling like this' to 'I can stand feeling like this without liking it in order to finish this project'. By practising this imagery technique several times daily for about a month, David was able to eventually feel only mild irritation when contemplating or actually carrying out a boring or unpleasant task.

David also agreed to carry out a survey among his work colleagues on their attitudes towards undertaking boring tasks. He discovered that those who met their deadlines had a 'It's got to be done whether I like it or not' attitude while those, like himself, who procrastinated had LFT attitudes: 'I can't be bothered to do it or put up with the frustrations unless someone puts a gun to my head' said one of his colleagues. As David tackled his workplace tasks, he said he saw himself moving out of the 'LFT camp' and towards the 'get on with it lot'. Reading Paul Hauck's book on developing self-discipline, *How To Do What You Want To Do*, helped to accelerate this process.

When David was less emotionally disturbed, he bent his mind to tackling the avoided workplace projects and was now able to focus on absorbing practical problem-solving tips. Some examples: he left a message on his desk that could not escape his eye, 'I have committed myself to getting rid of my procrastination – there will be no more excuses!' He divided his work into three categories: pending (no immediate action required); paramount (immediate action required) and projects (time to be allotted every day to these in order to meet deadlines). David was encouraged to keep a daily time log and note down every thirty minutes what he had done in that time. The purpose of the time log was to discover how he spent and, more importantly, how he wasted his time, e.g. long phone calls, too much chit-chat with some colleagues, handling paperwork several times without doing anything constructive with it, allowing frequent interruptions in order to 'distract myself from my dull endeavours'. Through such tasks, David's time-wasting activities reduced and his level of self-discipline increased. Eventually, David was able to manage his time and himself more effectively in the service of his goals (for a detailed discussion of time management, see Chapter 4).

During the course of coaching, David sometimes procrastinated about tackling his procrastination, i.e. he delayed addressing his delaying activities; therefore, a system of self-reinforcement was initiated. This involved rewards and penalties. David rewarded himself with such pleasures as an excellent claret in the evening for carrying out usually avoided tasks while he penalized himself with extra DIY chores at home when he 'slid back' at work. After eight sessions David was ready to terminate coaching:

MICHAEL: Do you want sum up what you've learnt about tackling your procrastination?

DAVID: Well, it seems so obvious in retrospect. I can carry out a task which is unpleasant or boring whether I'm motivated or not. Action is more important than the motivation. I now meet my deadlines despite some of the projects I'm assigned still being as dull as ditchwater.

MICHAEL: I'm happy to hear you're meeting your deadlines. What about the crucial problem of how upset you got, often very angry, when you had to do something that was highly boring?

DAVID: That was the real killer or so it seemed at the time. I used to be very apprehensive about experiencing that feeling, so as soon as I got worked up and convinced myself that I couldn't stand feeling that way – good old LFT – then I threw in the towel. Now I've learnt how to put up with it, the anger seems to have gone because I now tell myself something very different.

MICHAEL: Which is . . .?

DAVID: Well, if tasks are boring or unpleasant, so what? Get on and do them. I still get flashes of anger sometimes though.

MICHAEL: That's to be expected as progress does not occur in a smooth, straight line. Obviously it's not just putting up with boring or unpleasant things for their own sake, but if to do so helps you to achieve your goals.

DAVID: Oh, I understand that. I've been trying to convey that message to some of my colleagues who miss their deadlines for the same reasons I used to.

MICHAEL: Any luck?

DAVID: Not yet.

MICHAEL: But you've got the message loud and clear, I trust.

DAVID: Definitely.

Follow-up sessions were arranged for three, six and twelve months' time to determine if David had maintained his gains from coaching. David could contact me if he encountered serious problems within this time period and could not solve them on his own.

CONCLUSION

To change a behaviour pattern like procrastination 'requires *work*, and typically lots of it. Ironic as it may seem, the problem of avoiding work can be only solved by doing *more work*' (Knaus, 1993, section 2: 37; italics in original). This involves uncovering and then disputing forcefully those self-defeating thoughts and beliefs which insist that a task or situation is, for whatever reason, too difficult to face. By developing an anti-procrastination attitude, what appears to be unbearable eventually becomes bearable as action replaces inaction and avoidance.

Chapter 4

Time management

INTRODUCTION

Time is endless but your time is limited. Do you use it to your best advantage? Expressions such as 'There are not enough hours in the day', 'Where does the time go?' and 'I've got too much time on my hands' suggest not. These expressions indicate you are not in control of time: you keep chasing after it or are weighed down by it. On the other hand, you may know individuals who pack a lot of productive activity into each day and wonder: 'How can they do it and I can't?' But time is neutral: it does not tick faster on a busy day any more than it ticks slower on a boring or listless day, or favours one person over another. As with the other topics in this book, time management is about self-management; in other words, in order to understand why you do not make the best use of your time, look to yourself.

People who consult us for a coaching programme often tell us that their diaries are distressingly full, nothing can be cut out and everything is equally important. We frequently respond to this 'I can do nothingness' by explaining the 80/20 rule (also known as the Pareto Principle): i.e. 80 per cent of the results are derived from 20 per cent of the activities while 80 percent of the activities yield 20 per cent of the results (Koch, 1997; Lakein, 1984). This explanation can be an eye-opener with people eager to know which of their activities are the 'twenty percenters'.

POOR TIME MANAGEMENT

Davis *et al.* (1995) list some indicators of poor time management:

- Constant rushing (e.g. between meetings or tasks)
- Frequent lateness (e.g. attending meetings, seeing clients or meeting deadlines)
- Low productivity, energy and motivation (e.g. 'I can't seem to get worked up about anything apart from pay day')
- Frustration (e.g.'I always seem to be at the beck and call of others')
- Impatience (e.g. 'Where the hell is that information I've asked him for? He's holding me back from getting on with my work')
- Chronic vacillation between alternatives (e.g. 'I've been scratching my head for weeks over this. Whatever option I choose is going to put me at a big disadvantage. I don't know which way to jump')
- Difficulty setting and achieving goals (e.g. 'I'm not sure what my role is or what is expected of me')
- Procrastination (i.e. continually putting off starting a task or activity. This may occur because you fear failing to do a good job or baulk at the effort required from you)

To this list could be added *inter alia*:

- Perfectionism (i.e. the uncompromising pursuit of exceptionally high standards, e.g. 'I will only accept one hundred per cent achievement; anything less is crap'. This may mean you go very slowly to avoid making any mistakes or try to avoid the task because you fear doing a less than perfect job. Perfectionism is often a cause of procrastination)
- Getting bogged down in details (i.e. you cannot grasp the main issues because of your over-attention to details – 'I can't help being a dot the i's and cross the t's type of person')
- Feeling overwhelmed by your workload – (e.g. 'Now I understand what being stressed-out really means!')
- Unassertiveness (i.e not standing up for yourself, e.g. 'I don't like arguments, so even though it's not my job, I'll do it to keep the peace')
- Little delegation of work (e.g. 'If you want a job done properly, then do it yourself')

Jason was always racing from task to task whether at home or work; to others, he seemed to have a busy and enviably full life. However, Jason felt he was just 'rushing around like a headless chicken. I do a lot but don't seem to achieve much or value what I do.' If he stopped rushing everywhere, stood still and took stock of his life, what would he do differently? 'Haven't a clue,' he replied. Paula worked in a job that provided little stimulation or stretched her capabilities (she was in danger of 'rust-out' rather than 'burn-out'). When I (MN) asked her what kind of work she would like to fill her time with she said, 'I don't really know.' These replies demonstrate that time was being wasted or mismanaged because both Jason and Paula had no real sense of purpose or direction in their lives. *The essence of time management is knowing what your values and goals are in life and making the optimum use of your time to achieve these ends.*

However, knowing what your goals and values are does not mean that time will automatically subordinate itself to your new-found sense of purpose. You will need to review how you use your time and phase out those activities that are not goal-directed. This process requires adopting new attitudes and behaviours and tackling those obstacles to change (e.g. unassertiveness, perfection-ism) in order to make time management a daily and lifetime reality rather than an intriguing but elusive concept.

MAKING CLEAR WHAT YOUR VALUES AND GOALS ARE

Values help you to determine what is important in your life. As Sichel observes:

> They are the silent forces behind many of your actions and decisions. The goal of 'values clarification' is for their influence to become fully conscious, for you to explore and honestly acknowledge what you truly value at this time in your life. You can be more self-directed and effective when you know which values you really choose to keep and live by as an adult, and which ones will get priority over overs. (1993, section III: 48)

Some important values may include: financial security, interesting career, high standards, loving relationships, good friends, keeping fit, treating people fairly, fighting injustice, family life, making the most of every day, travel, working hard. If you have difficulty identifying your important values, Hauck (1988) suggests the following exercise:

Imagine yourself on your deathbed reflecting on a full and happy life. What were the ingredients that made it so? You do not want to reach old age full of 'If only . . .' regrets about what you did not do or have as when, for example, the poet John Betjeman lamented not having enough sex in his life.

Another exercise is to imagine that you have a terminal illness and you will be dead in six months' time. What activities would fill these remaining months of your life?

Exercises such as these can help you to focus on what may be missing from your life or what, though appearing to be important, is, in fact, easily given up. When you have identified your priorities (e.g. physical fitness), these need to be translated into goals. A useful acronym to guide goal selection is SMART:

Specific – 'I want to be physically fitter in three months' time.'

Measurable – what is your present level of fitness? What indicators would you be looking for in three months' time to determine if you have made progress?

Achievable – is there a reasonable expectation that your goal can be attained? Do you have the resources to join a gym or the ability to work out your own fitness programme?

Realistic – are you really committed to this fitness programme given the fact you are not giving up cigarettes, reducing your alcohol intake or monitoring your diet?

Timebound – can your goal be realized within the allotted time? Are you taking into account your other responsibilities and activities?

The above example relates to a short-term goal of three months (obviously the time period will be much longer if the person wants to maintain his fitness). Longer-term goals may involve setting up your own business three years from now or moving to France when you retire in twenty years' time. Longer-term goals need to be reviewed regularly (maybe every three or six months: 'Am I still on track?') and revised periodically (maybe every year: 'I think my original goal is too ambitious given my current circumstances'). Ensure that your goals are in line with your values (e.g. if you value family life then your goal would be to arrive home at a reasonable time every day in order to spend more time with your children before their bedtime). Also, your goals should reflect the presence of something you desire (e.g. 'I want to finish this essay in one month') rather than the absence of something undesirable (e.g. 'I don't want to keep on procrastinating over finishing this bloody essay!').

MONITORING YOUR TIME

Having established what your values and goals are, the next step is find out how you actually spend your time. This is achieved through the use of a time log (see Figure 4.1). The best way to fill in a time log is to record each activity and the time taken to complete it *as it occurs*. A contemporaneous account of time spent will obviously be more accurate than a retrospective one. If this proves too difficult to do, then try to ensure that you record each

Date	Time	Activity
	9.00	
	10.00	
	11.00	
	12.00	
	13.00	
	14.00	
	15.00	
	16.00	
	17.00	
	18.00	
	19.00	

Figure 4.1   Example of a time log.

hour's activities at the end of it. The time recorded in your log should equal the amount of time spent at work (if not, then maybe you are not being diligent enough in filling in your log or something unusual occurred which you did not consider to be part of your daily work routine and therefore omitted it). If you leave filling in your time log until you get home from work, it is likely you will produce a distorted account of your working day (e.g. 'How long did that phone call take? I can't remember. I'll put down twenty minutes to be on the safe side').

A time log can cover every waking moment of each day (rather than just time spent at work) as you may want to undertake a time management review of every aspect of your life. Keeping a time log for one or two days will probably provide insufficient information for a thorough review of your time as you may not spot behavioural patterns emerging (e.g. procrastination, unassertiveness) or how often certain individuals encroach on your time. Keeping a time log will increase your workload in the short term but enable you to see where changes can be made so longer-term benefits can be gained.

DETERMINING TASK PRIORITY

To discover this, you can prioritize your activities in terms of their urgency and importance (Adair, 1988; Atkinson, 1994; Butler and Hope, 1996; Covey, 1989; Forsyth, 1994; Jones, 1998; Maitland, 1999; McMahon, 2000). Urgent issues demand your immediate attention or action while important issues are personally meaningful. Activities can be placed in four categories:

1   Urgent and important
2   Not urgent but important
3   Urgent but not important
4   Not urgent and not important

Category 1 activities include responding to crises and meeting deadlines. If you spend too much of your time responding to immediate problems you might be moving into the danger zone of high stress levels and possible burn-out. As Fontana observes:

> People who in their professional lives seem always to be at the mercy of circumstances are usually those who wait for things

to happen, and then *react* to them. People who seem more on top of things are usually those who see things coming, and *act* in good time to guard against them (or benefit from them). (1989: 59–60; italics in original)

Category 2 activities allow you to plan ahead (e.g. 'What steps do I need to undertake now to meet my performance targets in six months' time?') instead of being glad just to have survived the day at the office, to take preventive measures to reduce the frequency of crises and problems, and to develop balance in your life. Remember not to neglect these activities just because they are not urgent, otherwise they soon will be (e.g. you become run-down through overwork because you kept putting off implementing a 'less hours at work and more fun and exercise' plan). Jones suggests that you should 'aim to schedule 60 per cent of your time for proactive tasks, leaving the other 40 per cent available for reactive and maintenance tasks [i.e. keeping things running smoothly], as well as unexpected interruptions, which may occur anyway' (1998: 49).

Category 3 activities often include responding to the requests of others (e.g. 'I need your help to finish my report by Thursday'; 'Listen, can you chair that meeting for me, I'm so busy?'). As for category 1, you are reacting to events but these activities are not important in helping to achieve your key personal and organizational goals.

Category 4 activities involve looking busy (e.g. shuffling papers, hurrying to and fro, organizing your desk). You may convince yourself that endlessly revising your time management plan is an important activity when, in fact, it is time-wasting. Activities in this category are neither urgent nor important and should be removed from your daily schedule.

As indicated above, the majority of your time should be devoted to important (i.e. goal-directed) but not urgent activities (category 2). This emphasis on what is important to *you* may smack of selfishness, but we would suggest it is more accurately called enlightened self-interest, i.e. you put your own interests and goals first most of the time while putting those of others, particularly significant others, a close second (Ellis and Becker, 1982). If you feel directionless in life and your desires remain unfulfilled, what kind of person might you be at home and work? Being at your best is more likely to bring out the best in others.

PINPOINTING EMOTIONAL BLOCKS TO CHANGE

Using a time management plan to implement your priorities in life may seem relatively straightforward. However, what often prevents or delays implementation are emotional problems (Dryden and Gordon, 1993a; Ellis, 1972). For example, you feel guilty because you want to spend more time on your own interests and you believe your children will suffer as a result ('And that will prove what a bad parent I am'); you become anxious about the prospect of saying 'no' to a colleague's request for you to take on some of his work because this will incur his disapproval ('He'll think I'm uncooperative and start rumours that I'm a bolshie bastard. How will I cope with that?'); or you have a low threshold for tolerating boring or unpleasant but important activities and become angry when you have to do them ('Watching paint dry would be more interesting than trying to make sense of these damn figures!'). People who have read books or attended seminars and workshops on time management often fail to act on what they have learnt because identifying and resolving emotional blocks was not part of the content (Ellis, 1972). Therefore, a time management programme should ideally include an emotional management component.

BECOMING BETTER ORGANIZED

This is achieved through the use of written 'To do' lists with each task prioritized and given a deadline: for example, 1 = top priority (20 July); 2 = medium priority (mid-August approx.); and 3 = low priority (no deadline). High-priority activities reflect the 80/20 rule we described earlier: a high percentage of desired results is achieved by a small percentage of activities. Try to avoid all time-wasting activities as they add nothing of value to your work (e.g. too many tea-breaks, office gossip, phone calls to friends). If you have several top-priority tasks vying for your attention, do the most unpleasant or difficult one first; too many top-priority tasks means you are not discriminating enough between what is essential for completion today and what can wait; and finish one task before starting another, otherwise you might find yourself flitting between several tasks and doing each one suboptimally.

Obviously not all top-priority activities can be finished in one fell swoop because, for example, you need further information which will not be forthcoming for several days. When this information becomes available, then the unfinished task becomes a top priority for that day. If a task is big or complicated, then break it down into smaller sections and assign an allotted period of time to each section (it is usually better to overestimate the time it will take rather than underestimate it). Sometimes a confusion can arise between time management and task management (Northedge, 1990): if you concentrate on time then you may overvalue the hours 'I've clocked up' rather than what you have actually achieved (you may have spent two hours on a project but the productive portion was the first hour); on the other hand, if you overly focus on the task, you may let it go on for too long ('I've got to get it finished. To hell with the time!'). Obviously a balance is required between time and task management in order not to waste valuable time or engage in unproductive work.

Ensure that 'To do' lists are linked to the achievement of your longer-term goals (e.g. if you want to learn a foreign language, then schedule some time every day for study); a wall chart should help you to see this linkage in an instant. Also, decide which tasks you can delegate and ensure that the person given the task has the ability to execute it successfully otherwise you will have 'to clear up the mess' which will add to your time pressures.

Do not use your time management programme like a new toy and 'play' with it constantly so you become bogged down with planning your time in such detail that it militates against actually getting on with the work (as one person pointed out to us: 'Instead of becoming a means to an end, it became the end itself. It felt like wearing a straitjacket'). Take a few minutes to plan tomorrow's main activities before you go home and then on the day itself, get on with them!

PRIME PERFORMANCE IN PRIME TIME

To produce high-quality work, Mann advises you find out when you work best: 'Some people are "owls", who work best in the evening; others are "larks" who are at their most alert in the morning. Do the most important and demanding jobs when you are normally at your best' (1998: 144). Quick et al. (1997) call this working at your best internal prime time. Adair suggests that the majority of us are larks and 'any task requiring solitude, concentration and creative thinking is best done before 10.00 a.m. You can accomplish more with less effort if you programme important items at this high performance time' (1988: 68). Internal prime time requires uninterrupted time: 'A clear couple of hours when you can mount an all-out attack on a problem is worth two days full of interruptions' (Atkinson, 1994: 68). Therefore, let others know you do not wish to be disturbed, shut your door and put on the answerphone or ask for your calls to be held. Conversely, external prime time represents times of the day which provide the best opportunities for yourself and others to meet (e.g. late afternoons).

IS IT WORKING?

If your new time management system is working effectively then you should notice some of the following improvements: increased energy, productivity and motivation, greater sense of control, more decisive, proactive rather than reactive, not taking problems home, acting assertively, tackling procrastination and perfectionism, improved timekeeping. Above all, there should now be enough hours in the day to complete your most important activities.

COACHING EXAMPLE

Richard was a thirty-year-old married man with three children. He described his day at the office as 'keeping my nose to the grindstone. I don't seem to have time to think. Everything comes at me and I just get caught up in it.' He was unhappy with his style of work and home and social life were affected by his tiredness and irritability. He admired work colleagues who controlled their day in a way that he was unable to: 'They enjoy their life both in and out of the office.' When I (MN) asked Richard what he valued in his life, he listed five key items:

1 Doing a good job
2 Family life
3 Being fit
4 More time for social activities
5 Being seen as likeable and helpful

The next stage was to translate his values into specific goals. He said if he could 'crack the work problem then the other things [2, 3 and 4] would fall into place'. He said his goal was to 'manage things better at work'. However, this was an aim rather than a concrete goal:

MICHAEL: What specific things would you need to achieve in order to realize your aim of managing things better at work?

RICHARD: Well for starters, meetings ending on time, keeping phone calls to the point, saying no to colleagues when they dump tasks on me which are not really within my remit and keeping interruptions brief and fewer so I can spend more time on the really important tasks.

MICHAEL: Okay. Let's see how you currently spend your time

Richard's time log

Richard kept a daily time log for the next few weeks so we could get a clear pattern of his behaviour (see Figure 4.2). In analysing Richard's time log, it was obvious that some of his activities were incompatible with his goals such as meetings overrunning, spending too long on the phone, tolerating frequent interruptions. What lay behind his difficulty, for example, in finishing meetings on time as he had overall control as the chairman?

RICHARD: I suppose I need to be more forceful with getting some people to stick to the agenda and not ramble on.

MICHAEL: But what prevents you from doing that?

RICHARD: I'm not really sure. I suppose I want people to leave the meeting feeling good.

MICHAEL: But how would you feel if you interrupted someone and asked them to stick to the agenda?

RICHARD: I'd be anxious about doing that?

MICHAEL: Because . . .?

RICHARD: Because they might not like it.

MICHAEL: And if they didn't like it . . .?

RICHARD: Then they won't like me. I know it's pathetic but there it is: I like to be liked.

MICHAEL: Okay, it's nice to be liked, but at the expense of sabotaging your goals?

Date: 6. 6. 2000	Time	Activity	
	9.00	Telephone calls	(20 mins)
		Correspondence	(15 mins)
		Interruption	(15 mins)
		Telephone call	(10 mins)
	10.00	Meeting	(90 mins)
	11.00	Meeting contd.	
		Paperwork	(15 mins)
		Tea break	(5 mins)
		Fed up	(10 mins)
	12.00	Project	(15 mins)
		Phone call	(10 mins)
		Project	(20 mins)
		Interruption	(15 mins)
	13.00	Lunch (rushed)	(15 mins)
		Listening to colleague's problems	(20 mins)
		Urgent call from customer	(15 mins)
		Helping colleague with paperwork	(10 mins)
	14.00	Meeting	(75 mins)
	15.00	Meeting contd.	
		Writing report	(10 mins)
		Interruption	(5 mins)
		Fed up	(15 mins)
		Writing report	(10 mins)
		Phone call	(15 mins)
	16.00	Phone call contd.	
		Tea break	(5 mins)
		Writing report	(20 mins)
		Fed up	(10 mins)
		Interruptions	(15 mins)
	17.00	Writing report	(5 mins)
		Fed up	(5 mins)
		Phone call	(10 mins)
		Tidying desk	(5 mins)
		Staring out of the window	(5 mins)
		Trying to look busy	(30 mins)
		as manager still on premises	
	18.00	Going home	

Figure 4.2   A sample day from Richard's time log.

RICHARD: Well, I don't want to become an obnoxious bastard.

MICHAEL: If you interrupt verbose colleagues, then some of them might think that but what choices do you have at that point?

RICHARD: I can agree or disagree with them.

MICHAEL: How would you vote at the present time?

RICHARD: I would agree with them because they don't see me as likeable any more.

MICHAEL: Are you allowing them to define you instead of you making up your own mind about yourself?

RICHARD: I suppose so. I never thought about it in that way before. From that perspective, wanting to be seen as likeable is not such an attractive value after all but more of a ball and chain.

MICHAEL: And one that you can free yourself from.

RICHARD: Easier said than done.

MICHAEL: True, but, in essence, not being liked is only a big deal if you make it one. Give up seeing work as a popularity contest and you will be able to claw back the time you are currently wasting.

Richard realized other time-wasting activities were linked to his need (he admitted it was much stronger than a want) to be liked, e.g. delegating little work in case some of his subordinates resented it, staying late at the office to impress his boss, being a 'friendly ear' for others' problems. To combat his need to be liked, Richard's action plan was to internalize a philosophy of self-acceptance, i.e. to forcefully and persistently accept himself irrespective of how others saw him ('I don't want to become insensitive or selfish, but I will start saying "no" when justified and if others get funny about it, so be it').

Some examples of his new outlook included: with colleagues who frequently interrupted him, he pointed to the 'Do Not Disturb' sign on his door and suggested a later time when he would not be so busy; he did not break off from his work while conveying this information. While chairing meetings he emphasized how important it was to keep comments concise and pertinent to the agenda and 'verbiage was a waste of everybody's time as we all have busy departments to get back to'; meetings now took half their usual time and unnecessary ones were purged from his daily schedule. Phone calls were also kept brief and to the point. He no longer allowed others to dump their work on him, but he would advise them on how to do it or tell them it was their responsibility to carry out the task. He delegated much more of his work so 'I can focus on the essentials'.

Richard's bouts of procrastination over difficult or boring tasks were tackled by developing a forceful motivational statement: 'Getting the task finished is more important than whether it is pleasant or not, so get on with it!'. Time spent on paperwork was reduced by only handling it once (OHIO): every time he picked up a piece of paper he put a tick in the corner; more than one tick on the paper meant Richard was returning to it without making any decisions about it. His 'fed up' periods virtually vanished from his daily schedule ('That's because I feel I'm more in control rather than being or letting myself be controlled by events or others').

Richard said he got strange looks from some colleagues and when they asked him if 'I was alright, I told them the reasons for my new behaviour. Some of them have been supportive, others less so but they were the ones I used to let take advantage of me.' With more time now released, Richard was able to prioritize his day, focusing mainly on important tasks (i.e. being proactive) and less on urgent ones (i.e. being reactive). He made sure he took an unhurried lunch break every day and went to the local gym three times a week. He got home earlier in a better frame of mind and was able to enjoy domestic and social life without the overlay of work worries:

RICHARD: When I come to work now I really am focused on it. Being myself rather than needing to be liked has really cleared a path through my life. Decisions I now make are based on the priorities of the job not on my emotional priorities.

MICHAEL: Is self-acceptance now an important value for you?

RICHARD: Very much so. In fact, there are a couple of people at work who I now recognize as fellow sufferers and their time management skills are as bad as mine were. So I might have a word with them and see if they are interested in learning what I did.

MICHAEL: Good.

CONCLUSION

Effective time management does not mean that every second of your day is accounted for, but that much of your time is directed towards achieving your goals. Like any other change, you will need to monitor your time management skills on a daily basis to prevent returning to poor use of your time (in Richard's case, time mismanagement might indicate he has slipped back to his approval needs). As the time management literature continually reminds us, time is a precious resource and each second, minute, hour that ticks by can never be replaced. Therefore, use it wisely.

Chapter 5

Persistence

INTRODUCTION

Writing a chapter on persistence requires persistence on our part. After all, what is there to say apart from if you want to bring about change in your life or achieve a goal, then persist until the change occurs or the goal is achieved? End of story. However, in considering the nature of persistence, there are more factors involved than simply urging yourself to 'Keep at it' and 'Don't give up' or being reassured by others that 'Persistence pays off' (e.g. what prevents you from being persistent?). Persistence requires the development of a philosophy of endurance not just for today or next week, but for the long term. Some dictionary definitions of persistence include 'continuing obstinately' which implies behavioural inflexibility or unthinkingly pushing forward. We leave obstinacy out of our discussion of persistence because we want you to think and act flexibly in the face of changing circumstances as you strive to reach your goals.

One of the essential qualities for success and achievement in life is persistence. Yet we often want change without working at it – we like the idea of change rather than the actuality of struggling towards it. Why does a New Year's Eve resolution become New Year's Day irresolution? How many times have you wanted to stop smoking, lose weight, get fitter, make a career change, leave a dull relationship, or even take a trip up the Amazon? What stopped you from doing it? We would suggest it was partly the effort and upheaval in your life that this might involve. Even if you say you are motivated to change, this does not mean that change will inevitably occur. Motivation consists of three components (Arnold *et al.*, 1995):

1   Direction – what you are trying to do or achieve.
2   Effort – how hard you are trying.
3   Persistence – how long you continue trying.

You may know which direction you are going in, put in a lot of effort initially to get there but give up your goal because you lack the persistence to sustain the effort to reach it. Grieger states that goal-directed behaviour is a '24-hour-a-day, 7-day-a-week thing' (1991: 60). You may blanch at this 'extreme' view of what change entails but then you have ask yourself what you mean by a commitment to change. Butler and Hope suggest that if you want to break what you consider to be a bad habit (e.g. tranquillizer dependence, smoking, comfort eating) then be 'absolutely clear about whether you really do want to change. You will need to be motivated not only to break the habit, but in order to be able to persist' (1996: 275–276).

Many of the people we see in our coaching practice hedge their commitments to change with 'ifs' and 'buts' (e.g. 'I'm willing to put in the work if I can be sure I will succeed' and 'I do want to change but I'm worried how hard you expect me to work'). Thomas Edison famously remarked that 'genius is one per cent inspiration, ninety-nine per cent perspiration'. We take the lightbulb for granted thanks to his 'perspiration'. Perspiration or 'sweat-soaked' striving may not be an image of problem-solving that appeals to you; instead, you may look for a quick-fix solution to your problems or yearn for a magic wand to make them disappear. We sometimes ask people to calculate how much time they have wasted looking for quick and easy solutions and how much time it might have taken to actually tackle the problem. The usual answer is that the latter approach would probably have taken a fraction of the time consumed by the former, but even that admission does not stop the search for an instant solution.

THREE KEY INSIGHTS

In our coaching practice, we usually provide people with what we consider are three key insights into the development, maintenance and eventual improvement of their problems:

1   Human disturbance or upset is largely determined by our irrational (self-defeating) beliefs and ideas. This was pointed

out by Epictetus, a Stoic philosopher from the first century AD, who said that people are disturbed not by things, but by the views which they take of these things. In summary, you feel the way you think (see Chapter 1).

2   No matter how or when we acquired our irrational ideas, we remain upset in the present because we continually reindoctrinate or brainwash ourselves with these ideas and act in ways that strengthen them.

3   The only enduring way to overcome our emotional problems is through persistent hard work and practice – to think, feel and act against our irrational ideas.

When we discuss these insights with people and how they apply to their own difficulties, they often see insights 1 and 2 as psychologically liberating because they now view their problems within their control rather than ascribing them to external factors that they cannot change. However, the implications of insight number 3 seem less liberating because of the 'hard work' required of them to translate theoretical understanding and remediation of their problems into daily practice. This translation involves the negotiation of self-help assignments to be carried out by the person between sessions in order to accelerate the process of change as well as put the person in the driving seat (i.e. learning to become her own coach).

TRYING VS DOING

When we ask people if they will actually undertake these self-help tasks, a usual reply is 'I'll try' rather than 'I'll do it'. While this reply usually indicates that they will make an effort of some sort, it also denotes a lack of commitment on their part because they have not yet grasped the philosophical implications of what real change actually requires from them – persistent and forceful action. They may have been trying for some considerable time to overcome a problem, but often to no avail. So when they come to us for coaching, we ask them if they want to continue with the same attitude that has so far proved unproductive. If people do not carry out their agreed self-help assignments, we persist in finding the reasons for their non-compliance as well as seeking ways to overcome it (Neenan and Dryden, 2000).

We communicate to people the difference between trying and doing by asking them for example: 'When this session is finished, will you try to leave the room or will you do it? Did you try to get dressed this morning or did you do it?' Doing gets results but trying does not. If some people are still unclear about what we are driving at, we may offer them a book and ask them to try and take it. If someone takes it, we remind them the task was to try and take it, not take it. By this time, the point has usually sunk in and a 'doing' outlook starts to become part of their daily life (to emphasize this point, you may wish to add mentally the initial 'D' to your name, e.g. Jane D. Brown). Next time you say 'I'll try' with regard to desired changes in your life, consider if it will really galvanize you not only into action but also sustained action.

THE MEANING OF WILL-POWER

Sometimes we are puzzled why people who declare that they possess 'will-power' fail to achieve their goals . . . until we analyse their definitions of will-power. Often these revolve around the determination to change but stop there (e.g. 'I'm determined to lose weight. It's just a matter of having will-power and then everything falls into place'). As Ellis points out, will-power is easy to invoke but difficult to put into practice because it is not only 'the determination to change but the determination to *work* at changing oneself and the *actual work* that one does to follow up this determination' (1980: 22; italics in original). Does your conception of will-power include the points made by Ellis?

FAILING TO PERSIST

In our experience, some of the following reasons may account for why you either fail to persist in your goal-directed endeavours or sabotage your efforts at doing so.

- *Short-range hedonism.* This refers to seeking immediate satisfaction and pleasure at the expense of your longer-term goals (e.g. you spend more time at college partying than studying and thereby fail to get the necessary grades for admission to your university of choice). In order to reach your longer-term goals, you usually have to forgo some (but not all) short-term pleasures but, as one of us has observed, 'one of the hardest things for people to do is to work towards their long-term goals while putting up with short-term discomfort' (Dryden, 1994c: 19). Short-range hedonism usually involves wanting to avoid pain, discomfort, inconvenience, etc. even though you know that this outlook will block you from achieving an important goal (e.g. 'I know I should get myself into a rehab. centre and sort out my alcohol problem but it's just too much hassle at the present time').

Short-range hedonism stems from a philosophy of low frustration tolerance (LFT) whereby you agree that constructive change is desirable in your life but the work associated with it is 'too hard' or 'I can't stand working that hard'. Walen *et al.* suggest that 'LFT is perhaps the main reason that clients do not improve after they have gained an understanding of their disturbance and how they create it' (1992: 8; see above section on three key insights).

- *'If only I knew how it started.'* People often convince themselves that if they discover the causes of their problems (usually lying somewhere in the past), then they will be motivated to overcome them or they will be spontaneously cured of them. Believing that the solution to your problems lies in the past rather than in the present is what Grieger and Boyd (1980) call the 'past history trap'. Trawling through your past may give you some insight into the acquisition of your present problems but it is unlikely to provide a helpful guide to present attempts at problem-solving. Current problems are maintained by current ideas and behaviours, not past events. Instead of what was, focus on what is and how it can be changed 'so that tomorrow's existence can be better than yesterday's' (Grieger and Boyd, 1980: 76–77).

- *'How can I persist if I'm no good?'* You may want to tackle an addiction problem, for example, but you consider yourself to be worthless for having the addiction in the first place. With this self-image of worthlessness, you assume that attempts at change will be futile because you can only see the bad in yourself rather than the good that may come from your persistence. We would focus on teaching you self-acceptance (i.e. not judging yourself in any way, only your actions, e.g. 'What I did was bad which caused havoc in my life and I want to learn how not to repeat such behaviour but I'm not bad for doing what I did'), so that your persistence at overcoming the addiction is not undermined or continually called into question by your self-depreciation.

- *'I'm not me any more.'* This apparent loss of identity can halt the process of change in its tracks. Giving up familiar but self-defeating thoughts and behaviours can feel 'strange' or 'unnatural' as you work towards acquiring a more productive problem-solving outlook. This dissonant state created by the clash or tension between the new, emerging self and the old, 'clinging' self can lead you to give up trying to change in order to feel 'natural again'. These concerns are illustrated in this extract from a coaching transcript:

SANDRA: It feels very strange not reacting as much as I used to, you know, lashing out when people criticized me. I'm glad of course but that doesn't lessen the strangeness of it all.

MICHAEL: What's strange about it?

SANDRA: Well, it probably sounds silly to you but that lashing out, being defensive or whatever you want to call it, was part of me, my sense of who I was. I feel I've lost part of myself.

MICHAEL: Do you think you've defined yourself too narrowly on the basis of a particular behaviour you engage in?

SANDRA: Maybe. I can certainly see and have experienced the benefits of keeping cool when people criticize me. I like feeling more in control of myself.

MICHAEL: Aren't you still Sandra but with some welcome changes?

SANDRA: I suppose so.

MICHAEL: How do you think you will see yourself in six months' time if you persist with these changes?

SANDRA: I suppose these changes will feel more natural, part of me.

MICHAEL: And how will you view the old, lashing out behaviour?

SANDRA: I suppose that will seem rather strange and distant. I might even have trouble remembering I behaved like that.

MICHAEL: So what will you need to do if you want to make these changes natural and permanent?

SANDRA: Tolerate these strange feelings and see them as part of the change process. If I see it that way, then these feelings probably won't last for too long.

MICHAEL: Exactly. That's the way it usually works.

- *'Others must help me.'* Your efforts at change are based on demanding the support of others (e.g. 'If I give up smoking, then so must you. I can't hope to stop with you sitting there puffing away'). You put the responsibility for your change on to others (e.g. partner, parents) as well as blame them if you are unsuccessful (e.g. 'I told you I couldn't stop smoking if you didn't'). Demanding that others must 'hold your hand' will dilute your personal responsibility for change and reinforce your notions that you are too 'fragile' to go it alone or stick at it.

- *'I was born this way. I can't change.'* This view of the hopelessness of change is based on a confusion between predisposition (tendency) and predetermination (inevitability). People who develop addiction problems, for example, may have predispositional characteristics such as a low tolerance for coping with unpleasant feelings or frustrations in their life, being sensation-seeking and avoiding boredom, needing instant satisfaction, and displaying 'a pattern of automatic, nonreflective yielding to impulses' (Beck *et al.*, 1993: 39).

  The implication of predisposition is not to succumb to pessimism, but to employ greater and more sustained effort to overcome the problem or minimize the adverse impact it may have on your life. As Ellis *et al.* point out 'all behavior is multiply determined and, therefore, clients with strong biological predispositions to a specific problem had better work harder to maximize the influence of psychosocial factors' (1988: 23). Such psychosocial factors might include mixing with people who support your efforts at change and avoiding people or situations that might help to trigger a relapse. As Hauck states: 'Nothing can eat away at your resolve more quickly than someone who is always giving in to his pleasures and tempting you with all that you are fighting against' (1982b: 75).

- *'What if I'm not successful?'* This usually means that all your efforts at change will have been wasted if you do not achieve your goal. We would suggest that this attitude stems from your philosophy of low frustration tolerance (e.g. 'I can't stand the uncertainty of not knowing. I struggle every day to put in all this blasted hard work, then I don't get the promotion. Why should I put myself through that?'). You want a guarantee that your perseverance will pay off and as you know you cannot be given one, this provides the rationale for not pushing yourself. However, staying as you are will maintain the same staleness and predictability in your life that you want to change. You can see uncertainty as a challenge instead of being daunted by it and that working hard towards an uncertain future is more likely to bring some rewards for you and overcome the stasis in your life caused by your demands for certainty.

- *'I'm not making progress, so I might as well give up.'* This statement may reflect your disenchantment with change because you are not seeing *immediate* progress as well as reflecting your ambivalence about change. You may have declared in your mind that if nothing changes by the end of the week, then there is no point in going on. This reinforces your uncertainty about wanting to change (you might be getting pressure from others to do so). When attempting to alter ingrained behaviours, it may be some time before progress is evident or if there is some initial evidence of it, resist the urge to dismiss it as 'insignificant'. Change usually occurs in small steps rather than one giant stride.

    Having contradictory feelings about change (e.g. 'I want to, but. . .') does not have to prevent you from persevering with it. Being totally and irrevocably committed to change is not usually the stance of most people we coach; it is only a minority who square up to change with ringing declarations of 'going for broke' or 'burning bridges'. Doubt and uncertainty are the usual concomitants of change. If you wait patiently for progress to emerge and work through your ambivalence about change, then you will be less likely to give up.

- *Commitment to sunk costs* (Leahy, 1999). Sunk costs are the investments (e.g. financial, emotional, vocational) you have made in a particular course of action such as staying in a relationship that you consider to be 'dead'. You are reluctant to leave the relationship as this means having to justify these failed investments (e.g. 'Why didn't I leave much earlier if I wasn't happy?'). To avoid such painful self-scrutiny, you persist with your failed investments (i.e. you remain in the relationship). Another example: you are in a job you describe as 'really boring' but leaving it would mean realizing how much time and effort you have wasted (e.g. 'Ten years down the bloody drain!'), engaging in self-condemnation (e.g. 'I'm a miserable failure for wasting ten years of my life in this boring job'), and confronting the risk of an uncertain future as you start again (e.g. 'What if the next job turns out the same or I can't even get one?'). Your focus is on looking back to preserve or justify these costs rather than looking forward to new opportunities; in other words, you dig yourself further into the hole (e.g. staying in the boring job) instead of trying to climb out of it (e.g. looking for a more interesting one).

Rather than any further commitment to sunk costs, you can: (a) ask yourself what constructive lessons you can learn from those 'wasted' years to guide future behaviour; (b) re-evaluate your conclusion that those years were completely wasted (e.g. 'The job did pay the mortgage and other bills after all'); (c) consider that some measured risk-taking opens the way for a more exciting or interesting life than always 'playing it safe'; and (d) understand the reasons for your behaviour during those years (e.g. 'I was afraid of losing my safety net') instead of seeing it as stemming from personal failure and deficiency.

- *'I'm too old to change.'* This comment may be a mixture of low frustration tolerance (e.g. 'It's too hard to do these things at my age'), fatalism (e.g. 'If I get cancer through smoking or a heart attack because of my fry-ups, so be it. It's too late to stop now and anyway, I enjoy these things') and a genuine belief that at a certain age you are set in your ways and nothing can dislodge you from them. We would encourage you to assume that your ideas are hypotheses rather than facts and put them to the test to determine if any improvements can be made in your life (Ellis, 1999). You may find that stopping smoking, cutting down on unhealthy foods, regular exercise, pursuing social activities can add more vigour and fun to your perceived 'past it' lifestyle thereby giving the lie to the adage that you cannot teach old dogs new tricks.

- *Jumping from task to task.* We usually see people on a weekly basis for coaching, with them carrying out self-help assignments between sessions. Some individuals expect to be given a new self-help assignment in every session as they assume that 'one lunge' at a problem is sufficient expenditure of effort on it. In fact, you may need to spend several weeks or longer on a particular task before you start thinking, behaving and feeling differently. For example, after two months' work, you are now able to stay in an anxiety-provoking situation and discover that your fears have not been realised; up to that point, you always left the situation as soon as you felt anxious to avoid experiencing your fears. We would suggest that you establish a coping criterion before tackling your next problem (Dryden and Neenan, 1995). A coping criterion helps you to assess if you have reached the stage of managing your problems rather than mastering them. This assessment can be viewed along three dimensions of relative rather than absolute success:

1   Frequency – are you experiencing the problem (e.g. anger) less frequently than before?
2   Intensity – is the problem experienced less intensely than before?
3   Duration – does the problem last for shorter periods than before?

If the answer is 'yes' to all three questions, then focus on another problem but do not forget to keep an eye on the previous one because, if left 'unattended', it might become troublesome again.

- *Hidden agendas.* These are the covert but real reasons why some individuals enter coaching rather than the ostensible ones they state to the coach (or, in your own life, you may tell your partner that you want to repair your damaged relationship with him when, in fact, you are looking for a way to leave but guilt about making him miserable if you 'desert' him prevents you from doing so). Hidden agendas involve you working (or appearing to) on issues that you do not want to resolve. If we detect the presence of a hidden agenda, we suggest to the person what is 'really going on' (i.e. we are not focused on the real goal) in an atmosphere of unconditional acceptance of the person as a fallible human being – the person is not criticized for having hidden agendas and thereby is more likely to reveal them.

  In the above example, if you were able to persist with overcoming your guilt (e.g. 'I will contribute to but not cause his misery if I leave; his emotional reaction is primarily his responsibility, not mine'), accept yourself for pursuing a hidden agenda and understand the reasons for doing so, then you will be better placed to reveal your true intentions and end the relationship, from your viewpoint, on an honest note.

- *'Change looks after itself, doesn't it?'* You may believe that after a period of sustained effort at tackling a problem successfully (e.g. overcoming procrastination), your progress is maintained independently of any further efforts on your part. This is a recipe for relapse: old self-defeating thoughts and behaviours can 'creep back' and create further problems for you. In order to maintain your gains over the long-term, you need to engage in daily practice of your new thoughts and behaviours in order to deepen your conviction in them and simultaneously weaken your adherence to old, unproductive thoughts and behaviours. Once this practice becomes habitual, less effort will be needed for this monitoring function.

- *'I don't feel any different.'* You might complain that after weeks of persistent effort on your part, you still feel down in the dumps even though you grudgingly acknowledge that you are thinking and acting more productively. The seeming intractability of your depressed mood may convince you to 'throw in the towel'. We would urge you not to do this because emotions take longer to change than thoughts or behaviours (the reasons for this phenomenon are complex). You can liken the change process to a three-horse race (Dryden, 1995). One horse is called 'Behaviour', another is called 'Thinking' and the third is called 'Emotion'. The first two horses always pull ahead while 'Emotion' is a notoriously slow starter but does eventually catch up. So have patience, persist with the change process and you will start to feel differently as your mood improves.

- *Secondary gains.* This refers to individuals who 'have a "vested interest" in maintaining the status quo of the problem because of the "payoffs" that the problem produces' (Cormier and Cormier, 1985: 189). For example, you remain depressed because of the sympathy and attention you receive from others which you believe will stop when you get better; you fail to stop smoking because you fear gaining weight if you do, turning you into 'a tub of lard' and becoming an object of ridicule. In both examples, the perceived consequences of change are worse than the problem itself. If you are unsure why your efforts at change are unsuccessful, ask yourself some of the following questions to assess for the presence of secondary gains (Cormier and Cormier, 1985):

1   'The good thing about my problem is . . . .'
2   'Has my problem ever produced any special advantages or considerations for me?'
3   'As a consequence of my problem, have I got out of or avoided things or events?'
4   'What do I get out of this situation that I don't get out of other situations?'
5   'How does this problem help me?'

If you want to give up your secondary gains and see your efforts at change bear fruit, then you will need to address the ostensible problem (unable to stop smoking in the above example) and the real or core problem (fear of ridicule from others and your belief that being overweight means you are repulsive).

- *'I can see what what the problem is now.'* You may believe that 'seeing' what the cause of the problem is will automatically resolve it without any further effort from you. Insight alone will bring about the necessary changes in your life. Unfortunately, the change process is more complicated: insight plus forceful and persistent action equals enduring change. For example, you see that your self-worth is dependent upon the approval of others and the solution to this dependency is to value yourself irrespective of how others see you. Unless you put this insight into daily practice (e.g. being assertive when necessary, doing things that may incur criticism or rejection from others), it is highly unlikely that you will integrate your new philosophy of self-worth into your belief system (i.e. you believe it deeply and consistently).

- *Insufficient repetition.* Questioning your unhelpful ideas using reason and logic, examining your internal dialogue for cognitive distortions (e.g. mind-reading, all-or-nothing thinking), searching for evidence to confirm or disconfirm a particular viewpoint are important skills, among others, to acquire if you want to become a more effective problem-solver. To be adept in these skills requires a great deal of repetition: for example, going over in your mind like a broken record why failing at a particular activity *does not* make you a failure as a person (the principle of self-acceptance) or that you can stand carrying out boring or unpleasant tasks in pursuit of your goals (developing higher frustration tolerance). Repetition is necessary because it is unlikely that you will internalize information upon its first presentation (it might take dozens of presentations before it 'sinks in'!).

COACHING EXAMPLE

Paula worked as a therapist and wanted to write an article for a counselling journal (it would be her first attempt). She liked the idea of having the article published but was less enthusiastic about actually writing it because she kept getting 'stuck', became fed-up with the research she had to do to give the article an academic underpinning and with the amount of time consumed by working on it ('It's getting in the way of other things I like to do'). She was angry with her slow progress and seriously considered abandoning the project 'to get some peace of mind'. I (MN) asked her if she really would gain this:

PAULA: No. If I give up I'll give myself a hard time for being such a wimp. I do want to continue but . . .

MICHAEL: But what . . .?

PAULA: It's such a hard slog.

MICHAEL: It may be a hard slog but what attitude do you bring to the task that makes it even harder?

PAULA: Me? Nothing. It's just a hard slog. I'm not sure I understand what you mean?

MICHAEL: When you sit down to write the article, what attitude is in your mind that makes you want to give up instead of pushing on?

PAULA: Oh, I see. Well, 'I hate this hard slog. Things should be easier.'

MICHAEL: Realistically, given this is your first attempt at writing an article and all that goes with it, should it be relatively easy or hard, or even a great struggle?

PAULA: Put like that, it should be hard, not easy. I've obviously got a lot to learn about writing articles. I'd probably say the same as you've done if someone was complaining to me about the difficulties of writing a first article.

MICHAEL: What are the consequences for you of having this 'it's too hard' attitude?

PAULA: I procrastinate a lot or I'm looking for excuses to stop writing and do something more enjoyable. I concentrate more on how bad I'm feeling than on getting the article done. Of course, the finish date for the article just recedes over the horizon.

MICHAEL: So that attitude does not help you to persist with the article to get it finished within a reasonable time.

PAULA: Definitely not.

MICHAEL: So what attitude would be more helpful?

PAULA: Well, keep on reminding myself that it should be hard writing my first article or a second or third if I ever get around to it.

MICHAEL: It's not just sitting in a chair reminding yourself that it should be hard because then you might go and do something else as a reward for accepting this fact.

PAULA: Okay, that's true. Keep on reminding myself while I'm actually working on the article. Rewards come after I've done some work.

MICHAEL: Right.

To encapsulate this new outlook, Paula nicknamed herself 'Persevering Paula'. She allotted some time most days to work on the article. She finished it three months' later and sent it off to the journal. When she received a reply from the journal she became down-hearted: 'They've accepted it subject to some changes and improvements. More bloody work!' I asked her if 'Persevering Paula' was just going to be around for three months or lifelong. 'Alright, I get the point,' she said. She revised the article, sent it off and was informed that it would be published within a year to eighteen months:

PAULA: I'm pissed off again. I hoped it would be published in a couple of months so I can see the fruit of my labours.

MICHAEL: Some journals will fast-track certain articles but obviously not yours. So you will need to learn patience, of which one dictionary definition is 'tolerant perseverance or forbearance'.

PAULA: (*laughs*) Oh no, perseverance again! I suppose I could write another article while I'm waiting.

MICHAEL: Now there's a thought.

CONCLUSION

We have emphasized in this chapter the central importance of developing a philosophy of persistence in order to achieve your goals which presumably involve getting more of what you want in life and less of what you do not want. An aversion to or intolerance of persistence is likely to encourage you to give up on tasks very quickly and convince you that sustained effort is too hard to bear. The irony is that your persistence at not persisting is likely to create more problems for you in the longer term which will then require persistence from you to resolve them if you are to avoid being overwhelmed or your life made miserable by them. The next time you baulk at persisting with an activity that is important to you, remember that the consequences of not persevering with it are likely to be worse than tolerating the uncomfortable struggle of 'sticking with it'.

Chapter 6

Dealing with criticism

INTRODUCTION

'You're hopeless!' How would you cope if someone said that to you? Get angry, verbally or physically lash out, agree with the person, become depressed and withdrawn, feel hurt and sulk or, with poise and coolness, ask for clarification: 'When you say "you're hopeless", what do you mean by that specifically?' Why is it that criticism can bounce off you one day then apparently crush you the next? When we see people for coaching, one of the things that most of them ask us is how to handle and respond to criticism constructively (e.g. 'When my boss starts ticking me off, instead of listening I keep thinking "Drop dead". Why can't I focus on what he is saying to me? There might be some truth in it').

Being on the receiving end of criticism (even if it well-intentioned) can touch a raw nerve or leave you feeling vulnerable. As we have argued in other chapters of this book, it is not the situation itself (in this case, being criticized) that determines how you feel, but how you think about the situation or criticism. For example,

A = activating event – your friend says to you that you can be spiteful at times

B = beliefs and thoughts – 'She shouldn't say that about me. She's supposed to be my friend! It's like she's stabbed me in the back. I've been a good friend to her. What did I do to deserve this?'

C = emotional and behavioural consequences – hurt and you withdraw from your friend's company thereby shutting down channels of communication (sulking)

You may protest that you did not want to feel hurt and would not bring on yourself something you did not want; therefore, her criticism of you caused you to feel hurt. We would argue differently. You can think of yourself at B as a gatekeeper: you choose what to keep out or let in. Instead of rejecting her criticism you allow it in; then you have another choice regarding how you are going to process her comments (e.g. reflect on what she said to see if there is any truth in it and what your measured response will be, or bridle with indignation that your character has been attacked).

In the above example, you have let your friend's comments in and chosen to evaluate them in the following way: denying her freedom of expression ('She shouldn't say that about me'); insisting she should act in a way deemed appropriate by you ('She's supposed to be my friend!'); viewing her comments as an act of treachery – the ultimate betrayal ('It's like she's stabbed me in the back'); seeing friendship only in terms of what you have done ('I've been a good friend to her'); and considering yourself to be 'special' in some way so this should not happen to you ('What did I do to deserve this?'). Your thoughts at B reflect the theme in hurt: you have been let down or betrayed by another and you are undeserving of such treatment; in other words, you have been treated unfairly. Therefore, B, not A, led to C. Imagine looking at the same situation in a different way:

A = activating event – your friend says to you that you can be spiteful at times

B = beliefs and thoughts – 'I wonder why she said that? Maybe I've said or done something she's not happy about. The best way to find out is to ask her and clear the air. I am surprised by her comment though'.

C = emotional and behavioural consequences – annoyed but you remain in contact with her thereby keeping channels of communication open

A is the same but is viewed differently by you at B which produces new changes at C. Whether criticism of you is fair or unfair, you are still responsible for your reaction to it. Once this insight into emotional causation has been grasped, you can then decide if you want to continue to respond to criticism in a 'touchy' way or be robust in dealing with it. We now discuss some of the ways people upset themselves when they are criticized.

THE APPROVAL JUNKIE (Forward, 1997)

While receiving approval from others, particularly significant others, is a pleasant experience, believing you *need* their approval, you cannot survive or be happy without it, places you in a subordinate position. For example, Jennifer was afraid when her boyfriend was upset because he would not speak to her and this meant she no longer had his approval. As Forward says: 'The approval junkie's motto is, "If I'm not getting approval, I've done something wrong". Or worse yet, "If I'm not getting approval there's something wrong with me"' (1997: 167). Jennifer always believed it was her fault that he was upset, begged to be told what she had done wrong and how she could put it right in order to be approved of again (i.e. receive her approval 'fix'). I (MN) asked Jennifer what happened when her partner criticized her:

JENNIFER: When he says things like 'You're getting on my nerves' or 'You're no good in bed', I sort of collapse inside, devastated.
MICHAEL: What thoughts are going through your mind when you 'collapse inside'?
JENNIFER: It's always the same: he doesn't want me any more, he's fed-up with me.
MICHAEL: And if that's true, what does that mean to you.
JENNIFER: If he doesn't want me then I can't be any good.
MICHAEL: When you say 'I can't be any good', what does that mean about you?
JENNIFER: (*voice drops*) That I'm worthless.
MICHAEL: So is the formula something like this: criticism proves you are worthless while approval means you are acceptable . . . temporarily?
JENNIFER: That's right. I'll do anything for him to be acceptable again. Really pathetic, isn't it?

Criticism *per se* does not make you upset: the meaning you attach to it does; in Jennifer's case, criticism means she is worthless. As Eleanor Roosevelt observed: 'No one can make you feel inferior without your consent.' If you are an approval junkie, you continually give your consent to be made to feel inferior because you already believe it about yourself.

In order to wean yourself off your approval 'fix' and stand up to criticism instead of allowing it to crush you, it is important to internalize a philosophy of self-acceptance, i.e. never rating your-self, only your actions or traits (e.g. 'My behaviour may get on your nerves sometimes but I refuse to put myself down because of it'; 'You say I'm no good in bed. Well, there isn't much sexual chemistry between us but that doesn't make me no good – in or out of bed.' Decoupling your actions from yourself allows you to be problem-focused (e.g. 'What aspects of myself require some change and do I want to stay in this relationship?') instead of self-focused (e.g. 'What's wrong with me?'). We would argue that coping with and responding to criticism constructively rests on a bedrock of self-acceptance. Jennifer forcefully and persistently worked at accepting herself, warts and all (e.g. 'I can accept myself for desperately needing his approval, but it is something about myself which I don't like and which I'm determined to change').

She came to see clearly the differences between needs and desires. Needs are based on demands: what you believe you *must* have in order to be happy or see yourself as having some worth. This rigid outlook does not really make you happy or convince you of your worth because you are usually anxious about losing your partner's approval, depressed if you do and often self-hating for being so 'weak' (Dryden and Gordon, 1991). Desires are based on prefer-ences: what you would like to have but do not insist that you must have in order to be happy or worthwhile. Jennifer had developed new perspectives on herself, the relationship and her partner:

JENNIFER: When he criticizes me now, I no longer collapse like before. I ask specifically what it is about my behaviour he is unhappy with and then I consider if his criticisms are war-ranted. I also do the previously unthinkable and criticize his behaviour which unnerves him. In fact, he seems at times to need my approval but I don't want to play games with him like he did with me. Now I see things clearly, I will probably leave the relationship as it has nothing to offer me now. I've taken off my shackles which I put on, not him.

MICHAEL: Is it just the relationship you are seeing in a different light?

JENNIFER: No, there are other areas of my life like my parents or work colleagues.

MICHAEL: Because . . .?

JENNIFER: Because being criticized doesn't have to hurt unless you let it – it may sting at times but no more than that.

Jennifer's need for approval was based on a fear of disapproval and what that would mean about her. However, if you only fear active disapproval you would not be too concerned at mere lack of approval. Why? As Dryden and Gordon explain: 'Because not getting approval is not the same as getting active disapproval. In other words, a neutral response would be OK; it wouldn't bother you' (1993a: 66). If a neutral response did bother you, then it is likely you are interpreting it as some form of implied criticism (e.g. 'She's not bothered about me either way. What am I to her – a nonentity or something?') and therefore you conclude you are being disapproved of. You might be the kind of person who *has* to know if you are being actively approved or disapproved of before you can evaluate yourself (e.g. 'She likes me, I'm OK; she doesn't like me, I'm not OK').

REJECTION

While the fear of rejection hangs in the air for people who need the approval of others, being rejected can often be seen as the most devastating form of criticism – you are no longer wanted or desired. When John's girlfriend left him after five years together, he described the experience as like 'being kicked in the stomach, then thrown in the dustbin labelled "reject"'. He attributed his depressed reaction entirely to being 'dumped' by his girlfriend whereas, in fact, there are two phases to rejection. Firstly, someone else rejects you; secondly, you reject yourself (in John's case, 'Without her, I'm nothing'). As Hauck points out: 'We can be rejected by others and still not reject ourselves. It is when *we* reject *ourselves* that we get into emotional trouble, not when others reject us' (1981a: 8; italics in original). The harshest criticism came from John, not his departing girlfriend. She did list a lot of his faults but, as he admitted, she never called him 'worthless' (even if she had done, he does not have to agree with her evaluation of him).

John saw and accepted that he was really suffering from self-rejection (which is not to minimize the unhappiness involved in the end of a five-year relationship). The realization that his worth and happiness rested largely in his hands rather than someone else's, gave him the confidence to ask women out, handle rejection from them without rejecting himself in the process and eventually find a new partner.

DEFENSIVENESS

Defensiveness is a common reaction to being criticized. Instead of letting in and mulling over another's criticisms of you to determine if there is any truth in them, you may resort to rationalizing your behaviour (i.e. engaging in plausible but specious reasoning). For example, a friend of yours mentions in passing that you talk about yourself a great deal. Initially shocked, you quickly respond by saying that you only do it to start a conversation or fill in the silences, poke fun at yourself to get people in a lighter mood and add sarcastically: 'Of course, you never ever talk about yourself, do you?' If you were to face the criticism head-on and find some unpalatable truth in it, you may end up damning yourself (e.g. 'She's right, I do talk about myself a lot. I'm only interested in me. What a selfish bitch I am'). Even though you try to explain away your friend's criticisms (e.g. 'She's going through a divorce, so she's taking it out on me'), you gradually phase her out of your life because 'we don't have much in common anyway' instead of admitting the real reason: 'How dare she criticize me like that! I thought she was my friend; instead she turns out to be a snake in the grass.'

If you put aside your defensiveness, then you can engage in rational thinking, not rationalization. For instance, you now believe your friends can criticize you and even though you may not like what is said by them, you will listen to the criticisms and evaluate them dispassionately (e.g. 'It is true that I do talk about myself a lot and I'm aware that some of my friends and associates do, at times, avoid my company because of it') and decide on a course of action to initiate change in your life (e.g. 'I do want better friendships, so I will work hard to make them evenly balanced instead of largely one-sided'). Finally, you no longer equate your behaviour with yourself (e.g. 'I may act selfishly at times but that does not make me a selfish bitch, just a person who refuses to rate herself on the basis of her behaviour'). Such rational thinking can help you to be open to criticism without necessarily agreeing with it and to avoid acting defensively.

GETTING ANGRY

We often hear people tell us that anger is a natural reaction when responding to criticism – 'How else am I supposed to feel?' Often the ideas behind such anger run something like this: 'He shouldn't criticize me. That bastard should keep his mouth shut!' Brian felt angry with his boss when he criticized a presentation he had made: 'Who does that bastard think he is criticizing me like that? His presentations are not so hot. Maybe I should give him a piece of my mind.' I (MN) asked Brian if he believed in freedom of speech:

BRIAN: Of course I do. That's one of the important things about a democracy. What's that got to do with this issue?

MICHAEL: The relevance is this: if you believe in freedom of speech, why did you get so angry when your boss criticized your presentation?

BRIAN: Well, he was being downright unfair, completely out of order. I thought the presentation was alright.

MICHAEL: Let's assume for the moment that his comments were unfair, why isn't your boss allowed to say things that are unfair?

BRIAN: He damn well shouldn't say unfair things about me. He should keep his bloody opinions to himself.

MICHAEL: Aren't you denying him freedom of speech with those 'shoulds' and damning him in the process? You don't have to like or agree with his comments, but is he allowed to make them?

BRIAN: (*long pause*) I want to say 'No', but if I really do believe in freedom of speech, which I do, then the answer has to be 'Yes'.

Brian's restrictions on free speech in this instance are determined by his emotional disturbance about his boss's comments. By pointing out the conflict between his support of free speech and his dictatorial 'shoulds', Brian was able to develop a new perspective on his boss's criticisms: 'His comments may be unfair but he has the right to make them. He is my boss after all. I can listen to them without disturbing myself about them. I was wrong to call him a bastard for saying things I didn't like.'

Sometimes people can say or do things that appear to attack your self-esteem and you verbally lash out at them in retaliation. This is called ego defensive anger. For example, you pride yourself on always meeting deadlines but on this occasion you are going to miss it. A colleague pops in to see you and tut-tuts: 'Oh dear, your report is going to be late. Whatever next.' You reply angrily: 'Get stuffed!' Whether your colleague meant to or not, he has publicly revealed what you consider to be a 'weakness' – failure to meet the deadline. By attacking your colleague, you are able to put off painful self-examination (e.g. 'I'm a failure for missing the deadline. Others in the office will now see me for what I am').

The first question to ask is: would you have been angry with your colleague if you did not consider missing a deadline as a 'weakness' thereby making you a failure? Linking your performance to yourself is a 'part equals the whole' error in thinking – your behaviour can never define or equal you. By acknowledging this error, you can focus without self-condemnation on the missed deadline, what accounts for it and how to complete the report quickly and professionally (if you turn in a sloppy report written in haste, this will probably reinforce your self-image as a 'failure'). If some of your colleagues do indeed regard you as a failure for falling below your standards, you can remind yourself that they are also making the 'part–whole' error which is probably no more helpful to them when they reveal their 'weaknesses' as it was to you when you revealed yours (incidentally, management-speak these days likes to talk of 'development possibilities' rather than 'weaknesses').

HURT

We discussed hurt at the beginning of this chapter but would now like to expand on the concept of deservingness found in hurt. This occurs when someone has made comments or performed actions that you perceive to be uncaring (e.g. 'I don't deserve to be told that I'm holding him back after years of my support and loyalty to him'). No matter how much you love or respect someone or what you have done for him or her, there is no law of the universe that states that they cannot make unkind or uncaring comments about you or that you have some special status in the world that exempts you from receiving such criticisms. Sulking is the usual behavioural response when you feel hurt and one of its functions is to try and make your partner feel guilty for his 'hurtful' comments and thereby induce him to make amends for them.

Even though the world would probably be a better place to live in if considerate and caring behaviour was always reciprocated, unfortunately this is not the case. Accepting that your philosophy of deservingness is shared by no one else is the first step in developing a non-disturbed and assertive response to criticism (e.g. 'I don't like the way you speak to me sometimes but sulking is not the way to deal with it. I want to find out what's going on with you so we can improve the relationship. Now what do you mean by "I'm holding you back"?').

CONSTANT CRITICISM

You may know certain people in your life (e.g. colleague, boss) who constantly criticize you and, understandably, you may get worn down by it and even convince yourself that you must have some serious character defect to invite so much sustained criticism. Not so. These people are chronic complainers, whiners who

> gripe *ad nauseam* about anything and everything. Believing themselves to be powerless to take control of their own lives, these people firmly believe the world *should be* this way, or *should not be* that way, and that you and/or other people should do something about it! (Dryden and Gordon, 1994: 33; italics in original)

Raymond worked with a colleague who was a chronic complainer. He tried several strategies to deal with the problem which proved unsuccessful: ignoring the complaints, avoiding the complainer or trading complaint for complaint. In our coaching sessions, I (MN) suggested a different approach:

MICHAEL (*as complainer*): Your work is always poor.
RAYMOND: You think my work is always poor. In what specific ways is my work always poor?

[Raymond acknowledges the criticism and then asks for clarification of it.]

MICHAEL: (*impatiently*) What do you mean 'specific ways'? Your work is always poor. What else is there to say?
RAYMOND: I don't agree that my work is always poor but sometimes I do perform poorly which is true, so it would be helpful to me if you could pinpoint specific areas for discussion.

[Raymond decides what is true and false regarding the criticism and persists with his request for specific information.]

MICHAEL: Trying to be clever are you? Well, for starters, your phone calls.
RAYMOND: What is the precise problem with the phone calls?
MICHAEL: They go on for too long. You're never off that bloody phone.
RAYMOND: I agree that I do spend too much time on the phone with some of the customers, so what specific suggestions can you offer me to improve my telephone skills?

[Raymond puts the complainer on the spot by asking for advice.]

MICHAEL: (*irritably*) You either know what to do or you don't!
RAYMOND: I'm afraid that isn't a helpful reply. Maybe I could sit in with you on some of your phone calls and learn that way.
[As the complainer is proving unhelpful, Raymond models for him how to offer a specific suggestion.]
MICHAEL: There is always a smart-arse in every office. What's the point in trying to help you? It's not going to make any difference anyway.
RAYMOND: I'm sorry you feel like that, but I would appreciate any further complaints you make about me to be specific in nature and, if justified, are then followed by your constructive suggestions for improvement. Otherwise your complaints are a waste of time for both of us.

Following this new strategy, Raymond noticed a sharp reduction in the number of complaints he received from the 'complainer': 'Always asking him to be specific about his complaints was the way to deal with him. He's on somebody else's case now.' As Mann points out: 'Constant criticism invariably says more about the (jealous or insecure) source of the comments than it does about you' (1998: 59). We would suggest that with any criticism made against you, instead of making yourself angry over it, analyse the criticism by asking yourself two questions: 'Is it true?' and 'Is it false?' If it is true (e.g. 'I do drink too much'), then admit it without self-condemnation and decide if you wish to pursue a course of remedial action (e.g. reducing your intake of alcohol). If it is false (e.g. 'I definitely keep to the recommended weekly units'), then let the person have the right to be wrong about you without damning him for his errors of judgement, and then get on with something more enjoyable (Ellis, 1977).

OVERSENSITIVITY TO CRITICISM

In the above example, if you tried to convince the other person that he was wrong about your drinking patterns, why would you need to do that? Why can't you let the matter rest? You have made his error a problem for yourself. You may easily take offence whether criticism is intended or not (e.g. 'I don't dye my hair. What's she going on about?') and try to always put the record straight about yourself (e.g. 'Look I'm not a worrier just because I ask you if we are going to get there on time'), so that the general impression among your friends and colleagues is that you are 'touchy'.

Such oversensitivity to criticism stems from having fragile or low self-esteem, i.e. others' criticisms or comments are converted by you into some self-inflicted insult (e.g. 'No matter how much I deny it, I am a worrier. I'm such a pathetic wimp'). To combat this problem, stop insulting yourself on the basis of other people's remarks and accept that there are aspects of yourself that you do not like and want to change. By becoming much less sensitive to criticism you may find that some of it is actually helpful when you listen to it in a non-disturbed state (e.g. a friend tells you he used to be a 'worry-guts' and how he overcame it, like you can too).

SHAME

You may fear actual or potential criticism because your faults will be exposed to the scrutiny of others; this scrutiny will result in their likely disapproval of you. Shame results from social disapproval (this is why shame is often called a 'social' emotion [Dryden, 1997]). Beck *et al.* describe shame as

> an affect [emotion] related to a person's conception of his public image at the time he is being observed by others or believes he is being observed. His notion of his social image may be accurate or inaccurate; but if he believes that his image has been tainted, and he cares about the observer's opinion of him, then he is likely to feel shame. (1985: 156)

The crucial ingredient in the activation of shame is whether you agree with the actual or imagined disapproval of you by others. For example, you regard yourself as cool under pressure but you lose your temper at a meeting and storm out. Office gossip paints you as 'hysterical' and 'a loose cannon'. You feel ashamed because *you agree* with these descriptions of yourself – you have undermined your public image of 'cool under pressure' by behaving 'hysterically'. Would you worry about 'losing your cool' if no one else was there to observe it?

To tackle shame, it is important not to judge yourself on the basis of your behaviour (e.g. 'I did behave badly at the meeting which I regret, but that does not make me "hysterical", "a loose cannon" or any other degrading label') and to make self-acceptance independent of the approval of others (e.g. 'I can accept myself warts and all irrespective of how others see me'). You can put these ideas into practice by being open about some of your perceived faults in relevant contexts, in other words, challenging your shame-proneness thinking (e.g. 'I want to apologize to everyone at this meeting for my behaviour last week. I'm not sure why I went off the deep end like that – maybe I was under some strain at the time – but I will do my best to ensure that it doesn't happen again'). By internalizing a philosophy of self-acceptance, you do not have to maintain your public image at all times in order to save face or worry about falling below your ideal behaviour because it will no longer mean a loss of face.

THE INNER CRITIC

Your harshest critic is often yourself. Others may put the 'boot in', but when you give yourself a 'good kicking' your boots are steel toecapped. You observe yourself and pass judgements such as 'Can't you get anything right you stupid idiot?' or 'Try harder. You're always failing.' You may believe that such attacks on yourself will help you to get out of your current difficulties, but these attacks are usually counterproductive as they reinforce your negative self-image when no progress is made or setbacks occur. Your inner critic cannot be appeased because it is afflicted with self-prejudice (Padesky, 1993), i.e. your negative self-image (e.g. 'I'm a failure') is maintained firmly in the face of contradictory evidence that could discredit it (e.g. 'It doesn't matter how good I am at my job: I didn't get the promotion and that's what counts and that's why I'm a failure').

Once you realize how bigoted your inner critic is, start to answer back in a constructive and compassionate way:

INNER CRITIC: You're a failure. Just accept it.

INNER COUNSEL: If I accept it, then that means I'll keep on listening to you. You're no help to me.

INNER CRITIC: Stop running away from the truth about yourself.

INNER COUNSEL: Your so-called truth is destructive and will drag me down even further. I know what you suffer from, I read about it recently – 'it–me' confusion (Gilbert, 1997).

INNER CRITIC: What are you going on about? You're the one that's confused.

INNER COUNSEL: I can only accept *me* if I do *it* well. Because I didn't get the promotion therefore I'm a failure. That is a trap I now wish to avoid. From now on, I'm not going to label 'me' on the basis of 'it'.

INNER CRITIC: Another false dawn for you.

INNER COUNSEL: I prefer to see it as the beginning of my enlightenment and your eventual termination. I've listened to you for long enough.

To answer your inner critic, write down your self-attacking statements and challenge each one in a self-helping way. If you find this difficult to do initially, imagine your friend's inner critic and how you would help her respond to the 'charges' (e.g. 'Susan, how does the failure of your daughter's marriage make you a bad mother? Where did you get the power from to control your daughter's destiny? If you could control it, then the marriage wouldn't have ended?'). The start of this inner healing 'is to sort out our relationships with ourselves' (Gilbert, 1997: 119). Your inner critic survives on the oxygen of self-depreciation, so cut off its supply by learning self-acceptance.

PERFORMANCE EVALUATION

While your performance is continually evaluated in a variety of contexts (e.g. social, sexual), we will limit this discussion to work-based evaluation. This can occur on an informal daily basis through comments passed by your boss, co-workers or customers, or at a formal performance review (DiMattia *et al.*, 1987). Whether you consider appraisal of your performance to be fair or unfair, mild or harsh, how you think about the appraisal is the crucial determinant of your response to it. Some examples: your boss says your performance is generally good but points out some short-comings which you become depressed about (e.g. 'I haven't received a flawless appraisal. My performance isn't perfect. I'm a failure'); you receive negative feedback and conclude that you are unlikeable; and your boss makes abusive comments (e.g. 'You're no good. You won't make it in this company') which you get angry about (e.g. 'How dare he talk to me like that! It's character assassination').

In order to cope with performance evaluation, start with exam-ining your own evaluations (e.g. 'If I was performing perfectly, then I wouldn't need a performance review. As this is not the case, I should focus on improving my performance. Calling myself a failure will get in the way of that focus'). Receiving negative feedback and concluding that you are unlikeable on the basis of it are two separate events (external and internal) that you join together; even if your boss does not like you, it should not unduly trouble you as long as her feedback is objective (if it is not, you can point out to her the animosity informing her appraisal).

If you have a boss who makes derogatory comments about you, instead of responding in kind, accept that he can act like that (the proof? – because he is) and that you will not disturb yourself about his probable disturbance. Be persistent in attempting to shape his agenda into something resembling a performance appraisal (e.g. 'You keep talking in generalities which is, as you may know, detrimental to any performance appraisal. Now, again, in what specific ways am I allegedly 'no good'? If you cannot provide any examples today, shall we postpone this meeting until you can?'). By forcing him to 'put up or shut up', he may get the message that the performance review is his, not yours.

EXPRESSING CRITICISM

The shoe is now on the other foot: you are expressing criticism instead of receiving it. How would you cope if the other person was hurt or angered by your criticism? John's wife, Sue, asked his opinion of the new dress she was wearing to a party: 'It's a bit short, isn't it? It would look better on a younger woman and anyway, you haven't got the legs for it,' he replied. Sue called him a 'bastard' and stormed out of the room. She spent that night in the spare room. John felt very guilty for upsetting Sue and tried to make amends for it by taking her out to dinner and stating that the dress did suit her after all.

While John may appear to be the villain in this story, it is actually more complex than that. John's guilt stemmed from two conclusions: (1) he did something bad – 'I shouldn't have said those things to her'; (2) and he is a bad person for what he said – 'She's right: I am a bastard.' John is responsible for his feelings and his wife is responsible for hers. While his comments were remarkably tactless to say the least, they also triggered ideas that belonged to his wife (e.g. 'He's really telling me I'm old and unattractive. He wants some young bimbo who's got great legs') which then led her to feel hurt (e.g. 'Why is he being so horrible to me?'). If Sue had not felt so insecure, she may have said instead: 'What do you know? I look a knockout, so don't get jealous this evening if I get chatted up at the party.' Your comments can contribute greatly to a person's emotional reaction but he/she, not you, is ultimately responsible for it.

Having said that, do not get carried away with the idea that because people largely upset themselves, you can say whatever you like without a care in the world for their reaction. We strongly recommend that you express constructive criticism which would be:

- Judge the behaviour or performance, not the person (or, in the above example, the dress rather than the person wearing it), e.g. 'I want to comment on some aspects of your workshop presentation. This is not criticism of you'.

- Be specific and factual in your comments, e.g. 'Your workshop evaluations show that one of the main complaints was not enough time for questions'.

- Do not dwell on past mistakes or behaviour but focus on how present changes will bring future improvements, e.g. 'Time for questions is usually an essential part of a workshop for gaining feedback on how well people are digesting the material and what adjustments may be needed to the content and pacing of the workshop. Does that sound reasonable to you?'

- Listen attentively so that you can discern if the person has any difficulties with or objections to the proposed changes, e.g. 'You seem hesitant about implementing these changes. Do you foresee any difficulties that I have overlooked?'

- Acknowledge that you have heard and understood what has been said to you, not merely the words themselves but the *meaning* of them, e.g. 'I appreciate some of your worries about these changes but, if I hear you right, you don't want to do any more workshops until you've done some training in workshop presentations. You're fed-up with being thrown in at the deep end. Does that seem an accurate summary?'

- Express yourself assertively, i.e. without diffidence or anger and attempt to achieve a satisfactory outcome or compromise for both parties, e.g. 'In order to improve your workshop performance and increase audience satisfaction, I will arrange some workshop training for you. Then we can assess the impact of the training on your future workshops and discuss any further difficulties that may have arisen' (see Chapter 7 for a discussion of assertiveness).

As Dryden and Gordon point out:

> Criticizing someone's performance or behaviour is not an end in itself; constructive criticism has a goal. That goal is to change the way a job is being done, or to change some aspect of a person's performance, or to bring about a change in behaviour. (1994: 57)

The next time you express criticism of someone, ask yourself if you have that goal in mind. Calling a colleague 'a lazy sack of shit' for not pulling his weight in the office would suggest not.

CONCLUSION

Criticism of you is inevitable; even Mother Teresa did not escape scot-free (see Hitchens, 1995). The important question is how to respond to it without disturbing yourself about it. We would suggest that you: learn self-acceptance by not judging yourself on the basis of your behaviour, only evaluate your behaviour or attitudes; assess the degree of truth in each criticism of you and do not be afraid to admit your mistakes or shortcomings; and then consider what changes you need to make to achieve your desired improvements. Constructive criticism can help your self-development; so welcome it.

Chapter 7

Assertiveness

INTRODUCTION

Assertion training has been most closely associated with behaviour therapy (Salter, 1949; Wolpe, 1958; Wolpe and Lazarus, 1966). In the 1970s, assertion training developed cognitive components because '(1) changing people's ideas influences their assertive behavior, and (2) changing people's behavior leads to changes in their ideas' (Grieger and Boyd, 1980: 187). Outside of therapy, learning to be assertive has become a popular form of self-development, having been launched into the public realm in 1970 by Alberti and Emmons with their book *Your Perfect Right*. Since then, a large self-help literature has been spawned (e.g. Alberti and Emmons, 1975; Dickson, 1982; Dryden, 1994a; Dryden and Gordon, 1994; Ellis, 1977; Forward, 1997; Hauck, 1981b; Lazarus and Fay, 1975; Mansfield, 1994; Smith, 1975).

Assertion training is an important element in tackling, among other problems, anger (Dryden, 1990), anxiety (Blackburn and Davidson, 1995), depression (Beck *et al.*, 1979), and substance abuse (Beck *et al.*, 1993), as well as being employed in couple and group counselling (respectively, Ellis *et al.*, 1989; Palmer and Dryden, 1995).

Assertion training 'has been addressed particularly to women who have internalised social expectations of meekness and self-denial' (Feltham and Dryden, 1993: 12) and who are traditionally over-represented in therapy. Wolfe states that assertion training 'constitutes a major remediation for female's passive and dependent behaviors . . .' by replacing '. . . their habits of learned helplessness with those designed to increase personal effectiveness' (1985: 107). Politically, assertiveness can be seen as a form of advocacy that attempts to tackle marginalization, injustice, oppression and inequality, at the individual, group or societal level.

Historically, assertion training focused on helping individuals to stand up for themselves in situations of actual or potential conflict but 'for some time now . . . has been extended to include the expression and accurate communication of *affectionate* behaviour, where appropriate. Thus assertive behaviour now encompasses the expression of positive as well as of negative feelings' (Nelson-Jones, 1995: 225–226; italics in original). You may be able to express negative feelings to a colleague (e.g. 'It does get on my nerves when you keep on interrupting me. I wish you wouldn't do it') but stumble over expressing positive feelings to your partner (e.g. 'I, er, would like to, er, say how much I, um . . . well, sort of feel towards you if . . . if you know what I'm getting at'). In the latter case, you may be reluctant to express your feelings in case they are not reciprocated thereby confirming in your mind your lack of self-worth. We would also add acceptance of one's faults and limitations without self-condemnation to the discussion of assertiveness.

DISTINGUISHING BETWEEN ASSERTION, AGGRESSION AND UNASSERTIVENESS

Understanding the differences between these three concepts is the 'first step in teaching the client to behave more assertively' (Walen *et al.*, 1992: 295). This phase is often called discrimination training. Hauck defines assertion 'as standing up for one's rights *without* anger' and aggression 'as standing up for one's rights *with* anger' (1991a: 207; italics in original). When you act assertively you recognize that the other person has rights also and you hope to achieve a satisfactory result for both sides (a 'win–win' outcome; see Box 7.1).

Aggression involves you acting in an intimidating, demeaning, controlling, manipulating or demanding manner. Only your rights count – your aim is to come out on top at the expense of the other person (a 'win–lose' outcome). Jakubowski and Lange (1978: 69–70) list nine beliefs that promote aggressive behaviour:

- I must win in order to be OK.
- If I don't come on strong, I won't be listened to.

> *Box 7.1*   Some assertive rights
>
> The right to say 'no'
> The right to make mistakes
> The right to consider my needs important
> The right to express my feelings in an appropriate manner without
>   violating anybody else's rights
> The right to take responsibility for my actions
> The right not to be understood
> The right to set my own priorities
> The right to respect myself
> The right to be me
> The right to be assertive without feeling guilty
>
> (Source: Palmer and Dryden, 1995)

- The world is hostile, and I must be aggressive in order to make it.
- To compromise is to lose.
- I must make an impact.
- I must get my way.
- Aggression is the only way to get through to some people.
- I must prove I'm right and they're wrong.
- The world must be fair; it's intolerable when people mistreat me.

So when you engage in what you assume is assertive behaviour, is your intent to offer your opinion to others or force it on them? And is the outcome likely to be some sort of compromise or the humiliation of the other person?

Unassertiveness 'involves violating one's own rights by failing to express honest feelings, thoughts, and beliefs, or expressing one's thoughts and feelings in such an apologetic, diffident, self-effacing manner that others can easily disregard them' (Lange and Jakubowski, 1976: 9). The message often conveyed by your unassertiveness is: 'I don't really count; what others want is much more important.' Unassertiveness can appear in the guise of politeness (Lange and Jakubowski, 1976), e.g. 'Politeness is an expression of good manners and avoids unpleasantness'. However, your internal self-talk might not be so 'polite' as you berate yourself for failing to say what was really on your mind. It is important in assessing unassertiveness to determine if it is a trait (i.e. part of your personality) or situation-specific (e.g. only with your boss) as this will give an indication of the extent of your interpersonal difficulties.

At first blush, aggression and unassertiveness seem very different behavioural approaches to tackling problematic situations yet they have something in common: both are based on a threat to a person's self-esteem. For example, you avoid conflict with your partner because this might lead to the withdrawal of his approval, confirming in your mind your worthlessness; a colleague criticizes some of your proposals and, instead of a constructive discussion, you verbally lash out in order to 'crush' her and prove how strong you are – accepting some of her criticisms would prove you are a wimp. If you are unassertive and admire someone else's frequent displays of anger because it suggests they have the strength of character that you lack, think again – both of you are suffering from low self-esteem.

MISCONCEPTIONS ABOUT ASSERTIVENESS

Assertion training is a popular method for gaining greater self-confidence and control over your life and thereby reducing or removing previous feelings of helplessness and hopelessness. As Beck *et al.* point out, self-assertion is 'an effective antidote to depression' (1979: 83). However, you may misconstrue the role of assertion in your life and therefore subscribe to some of the following ideas.

Acting assertively means that you automatically get what you want

By acting assertively, you may get what you want but there is no guarantee. Other people may be indifferent or hostile to your declaration of your rights as they may see them as an infringement or negation of their own rights (e.g. 'Look, if I turn my music down because it's too loud for you, then I won't be able to enjoy it. So get lost'). In this situation, compromise is not possible (e.g. you may have to get the police or local council to enforce your 'right to a quiet life'). Therefore, be realistic about the limits of your newly acquired assertiveness, otherwise you can quickly slip into anger and resentment when people do not respond in the hoped-for way.

Having become assertive, you must act in this manner all of the time

Being assertive also means being prudent: undesirable consequences may be avoided if you remain silent or take a low-key
approach in certain situations (e.g. going to your partner's parents
for Sunday dinner in order to avoid a prolonged row if you refuse
to). Therefore, 'in some instances, discretion may be the better part
of assertion' (Walen *et al.*, 1992: 294–295). Assertiveness is one
option among others and not an automatic reflex in every situation
where you feel thwarted or challenged in some way. Being continually 'rights conscious' can lead to exasperation of your colleagues, partner or friends and result in what Robb calls an
'assertive backlash' as individuals 'find themselves fired, divorced
or otherwise disenfranchised' for speaking up (1992: 265; see Robb
for a discussion of presumed rights in assertiveness training). One
vision of hell may be living or working with people who will not be
denied on any issue.

Being assertive will make people respect or like you (Ellis, 1979)

In fact, domestic, social and work relationships may become
increasingly fraught as you begin to assert yourself (e.g. 'It's about
time I got some things off my chest') and may even end in rejection
(e.g. 'I thought she would respect me more, not leave me'). Instead
of an anticipated greater interpersonal closeness, others pull back
and maintain a wary distance.

Being assertive always equals strength (Ellis, 1979)

From this perspective, unassertiveness always equals weakness and
therefore you become compulsively assertive to avoid being
perceived as weak or inferior by others (e.g. 'I'm never going back
to my "being a doormat" days'). Ironically, you are displaying
'weakness' by not allowing yourself to choose when assertion is the
best option in a particular situation because you are overly worried
about the opinions of others – you are a slave to your perceived
public image.

Being assertive makes you a good person

Assertiveness will probably help you to become adept at getting more of what you want and less of what you do not want; what it will not do is to make you an intrinsically good, better or superior person. Basing your self-worth on a particular behaviour can quickly lead to self-depreciation when you lapse into unassertiveness or find assertiveness 'isn't working' (e.g. 'Why aren't people listening to me? It must mean I'm no good again').

Being assertive will solve all your problems

It will undoubtedly help towards solving some of your problems but is certainly not a cure-all. As one person said to me (MN) in a disillusioned tone, 'I thought going on an assertiveness course would transform my life and my problems'. In addition to assertiveness, we would suggest, *inter alia*, learning self-acceptance in the face of setbacks and being persistent in order to reach your goals are also important qualities to acquire.

BLOCKS TO ASSERTIVENESS

What prevents you from being assertive? Hauck (1981b) advances five fears:

1   Fear of injury – e.g. physical violence may be threatened or unleashed in order to keep you in thrall (e.g. trapped in an abusive relationship).
2   Fear of failure – e.g. not starting one's own business because it could go wrong and the 'catastrophic' consequences that would follow.
3   Fear of hurting other people's feelings – e.g. 'If I tell him that he doesn't satisfy me in bed, I will humiliate him, crush him. I'd feel very guilty for doing that to him.'
4   Fear of rejection – e.g. continually trying to please others because you believe that not having their love or approval would be devastating (e.g. 'I'd be worthless without her love').
5   Fear of financial insecurity – e.g. you stay in a boring job because you are worried about financial instability and potential hardship if you leave it.

Trower *et al.* (1988) suggest:

1   Damning anger – your style of thinking leads you to damn others for frustrating you in some way. Your intention is to hurt or insult others in your interactions with them rather than focusing on trying to get what you want – for example, 'You're a lazy bastard' as opposed to 'I would like to discuss with you a more equal distribution of work around the house'.
2   Guilt – you believe it is wrong to try and fulfil your own wishes because you may equate this with selfishness or, alternatively, you doubt whether you have or deserve any personal rights because you are not worthy enough.

Gilbert (2000) identifies:

1   Fear of counter-attack – when you have made your complaints, you fear being overwhelmed by the other person's response so that you become tongue-tied and blush, your mind goes blank, your words come out in a jumbled fashion, etc. and you end up feeling ashamed or humiliated. In essence, you will come off worst in any encounter.
2   Loss of control – assertion can involve physiological arousal which then might lead to behavioural or verbal disinhibition (e.g. shouting obscenities at your partner).
3   Self-blame – you blame yourself for causing problems or conflict when the responsibility for such problems lies with others (e.g. 'It's my fault that my husband hits me. I should stay quiet when he's in a foul mood').
4   Positive self and competitiveness – you view lack of assertiveness as having positive qualities of being good and caring; assertiveness is seen as selfish and pushy: 'To become more assertive threatens becoming similar to people they do not like, and losing a certain satisfaction with self that they are nicer than other people' (Gilbert, 2000: 158).

Lange and Jakubowski (1976) offer another major, but more obvious, reason for unassertiveness: you do not know how to act assertively because of a lack of role models or opportunities to acquire such skills. We would also include: cultural, philosophical and religious beliefs which, for example, emphasize deference, stoicism or self-denial; previous assertive experiences which have turned out badly for you and, therefore, you are reluctant to try again; unassertiveness being perceived as innate, i.e. a fixed part of your personality; procrastination, which allows you to keep putting off speaking up about your partner's behaviour and thereby avoiding the feared consequences such as being abandoned by her (see Chapter 3 on overcoming procrastination).

EMOTIONAL AND BEHAVIOURAL ASPECTS OF ASSERTIVENESS TRAINING

The first task is to identify areas of interpersonal difficulty in your life, establish goals for change and then undertake an assessment of your present functioning in those areas. As we have pointed out elsewhere in this book (see Chapter 2 for example), you cannot usually engage in behavioural skills acquisition while emotionally disturbed. Therefore, you will need to determine if there are primary emotional blocks to learning assertiveness (e.g. anxiety).

In addition, there may be secondary emotional problems to contend with (i.e. emotional difficulties that arise as a result of your inability to tackle the primary problem). For example, you feel ashamed of and angry with yourself for your perceived weakness in not challenging a friend when she does not repay a loan; unable to contain your frustration any longer, you verbally lash out at her, then feel guilty (tertiary emotional problem) about your angry outburst – 'I shouldn't have lost my temper with her. I'm bad for behaving like that.' You return to your unassertive state which then reinforces your reluctance to speak up again.

Let us now look at these emotional blocks in turn. First, your anxiety. You are worried that your friend will become angry when you ask her for your money back and reject you, which you will evaluate as 'unbearable'. Is real friendship based on exploitation? You only believe that loss of her friendship is unbearable because you label it that way. If you saw her rejection of you as unpleasant but bearable, this could motivate you to persist in asking for your money back as well as reviewing all your current friendships to decide which are worth preserving and which might be terminated.

Second, your shame. Not challenging your friend to repay the loan indicates intrapersonal difficulties that need to be addressed, not self-denigration as being 'weak'. If you see yourself as 'weak', how will this self-image help you to gain the confidence and strength to be assertive?

Third, your guilt. Your angry outburst confirms your status as a fallible (imperfect) human being, not a damnable one. The accumulated frustrations of being unassertive often erupt into anger; this is understandable, but it is better to address your frustrations constructively instead of letting them fester.

Often these secondary and tertiary emotional problems have to be dealt with first as they can interfere with your efforts to tackle the primary emotional problem. Once the emotional difficulties have been ameliorated, you can then focus on the behavioural skills you need to acquire. It should always be borne in mind that once the emotional problems have been ameliorated, your dormant assertiveness may, so to speak, reassert itself spontaneously.

The main behavioural methods in assertiveness coaching are role play, modelling and rehearsal before *in vivo* enactment. Role play involves a person playing himself and then switching roles to play the other person in the problem situation; I (MN) would play both roles alternately. Role playing enables the person to practise his desired behaviour as well as attempt to understand the other person's reactions to such behaviour. Role play also provides further information about the cognitive, emotive and behavioural difficulties in being assertive, e.g. the person makes poor eye contact because he believes 'I can't stand the way she looks at me with such contempt'. After role play, I debrief the client in order to deal with any issues that may have arisen from the exercise (e.g. the person says 'I'll never get the hang of this').

Modelling is used by me to demonstrate to the person how to act assertively and then the person practises such behaviour himself. The person is not expected to reproduce my behaviour but aims to improve his own interpersonal style in a way that is realistic for him. The person can also be encouraged to observe other role models, e.g. work colleagues, friends.

Rehearsal of and coaching in the new behaviour pays attention to its verbal and non-verbal aspects. Verbal behaviour includes direct, clear and concise statements using 'I' language and avoids personal abuse, condemnation or being too apologetic. With regard to the non-return of the money, you could say: 'I feel annoyed that you are reluctant to return the money I lent you. Please explain the reasons for the delay and provide a date when the money will be returned. I don't want this incident to jeopardize our friendship.' When being assertive with individuals who are oversensitive, we recommend you use an 'assertive sandwich because you sandwich what you have to say between two slices of affirmation' (Dryden, 1992: 95), e.g. 'I always look forward to your phone calls but please don't phone me after midnight. Any other time during the evening will be great to talk to you.'

Non-verbal behaviour includes focusing on body posture, eye contact, facial expressions, use of gestures, voice level and tone. A clear verbal statement can be undermined by non-verbal behaviour (e.g. excessive blinking, keep looking away, frequent swallowing) while para-verbal responses (e.g. ers, ums) can blunt the impact of what is being said.

A hierarchy of assertion tasks, from simple to more difficult, can be constructed to aid the person's desensitization to the apprehension he normally experiences in certain interpersonal situations. By gradual exposure to fearful situations, his apprehension is eventually reduced with a corresponding increase in his social competence and confidence. Such homework or between-session assignments in real-life situations provides the crucial feedback on his performance and any modifications to it that may be needed. He can reward himself each time he has carried out an assertion task in order to reinforce his new behaviour.

In your own efforts to be more assertive, you need to be alert to the presence of task-interfering cognitions (TIC; Burns, 1981), e.g. 'I'm being assertive but it's not getting me anywhere. This is not working at all.' TIC can be replaced by TOC (task-orientated cognitions), e.g. 'I have to keep reminding myself that being assertive does not mean that people will always respond in a positive way or agree with my views. Speaking up for myself is the important point.'

Behaving assertively can help to change or influence the way others behave towards you (e.g. your opinion is now sought whereas before it was ignored). Such external behaviour

> also produces important internal effects. That is, we are likely to think and feel differently about ourselves as a result of behaving assertively. By letting other people see, through our behaviour, that we expect to be treated as a person of worth we are also likely to affect our own evaluation of ourselves and what we are capable of. (Sheldon, 1995: 203)

EIGHT STEPS TO HEALTHY SELF-ASSERTION (DRYDEN, 1992)

Step 1: Get the person's attention

Obvious as this may seem, do not make important points while your partner is reading the newspaper or your colleague is working on the computer. Ensure that you have the person's full attention and distractions (e.g. the television is on, colleagues are close by) are avoided.

Step 2: Describe objectively the other person's behaviour that you have difficulty with

This means you describe the difficulty without personalizing it, making accusations or interpretations (e.g. 'You deliberately read the paper when you knew I wanted to talk to you. We're growing further apart and you don't care') and stick to the facts (e.g. 'I said I wanted to speak to you and you picked up the paper and started reading it'). As well as being objective, make sure your comments are short otherwise the other person might mentally 'drift off'.

Step 3: Express constructive feelings

We would suggest that disappointment and annoyance are constructive feelings to express to your partner or colleague while anger, hurt and jealousy would probably undermine your attempts at being assertive (e.g. if you are angry, you are more likely to unleash your pent-up frustrations, 'We're growing apart and you don't give a damn!'). Use 'I feel' statements to take responsibility for your feelings (e.g. 'I feel annoyed that you would rather read the paper than talk to me') instead of 'You make me feel' statements which then place responsibility for your feelings on to the other person (as we have argued throughout this book, our feelings are largely self-created).

Step 4: Check your interpretations and invite a response

You described your partner's behaviour objectively at step 2 but what you really want to convey is your interpretation of his behaviour. Interpretations are not facts, so do not frame them as facts (e.g. 'You know we're growing apart') and invite a response to encourage a discussion of the issue (e.g. 'It seems to me, we're growing further apart and you don't appear to care. What do you think about this?').

Step 5: Listen to the other person's response and give feedback

Listening means in an open-minded way instead of dismissing your partner's replies as soon as they are given (e.g. 'Do you expect me to believe that?'). Listen carefully to what he says (e.g. 'I suppose I'd rather read the paper because you keep on about this issue. I don't know where you get the idea from that we're growing apart. If we were, I would care') and then offer your feedback. If you are satisfied with the reply, then say so; if you are not satisfied, then express your doubts without attacking the other person (e.g. 'I'm not convinced by your reply: it's not just reading the newspaper, you spend so much time doing things that don't include me').

Step 6: State your preferences clearly and specifically

Your preferences (not demands, e.g. 'You must do this') are based on what you want from the other person and should be stated in a clear and concrete way (e.g. 'I would like you to take me out at least once a week'). You can also point out the positive consequences that are likely to occur (e.g. 'I really think it will bring us closer together').

Step 7: Request agreement from the other person

If your partner agrees to your proposal, then work out the details (e.g. Wednesday night will be 'our going out together' night). If your partner disagrees, ask him what changes he is prepared to make. If he is not prepared to make any changes (e.g. 'Why should I change because of your problem') and this is a key area of relationship dissatisfaction for you, then you need to consider carefully the pros and cons of staying in the relationship.

Step 8: Communicate any relevant information concerning future episodes

This means telling the other person what you will you do if the problem re-occurs (e.g. 'If I feel we are drifting apart again, I will bring it to your immediate attention'), ask the other person in what manner he would like you to respond (possible reply: 'Just tell me in a calm way without jumping up and down about it') and ask him what he will do differently in future to deal with the situation (possible reply: 'Well, if for any reason going out at least once a week starts to fall off, then I will know something is wrong and it will be "state of the relationship" time again').

COACHING EXAMPLE

Carol was a 30-year-old woman who said she felt trapped in a relationship that she desperately wanted to leave. She described her partner as 'a heavy drinker, he's got no ambition, he's no fun to be with any more, and he spends most of his time stuck in front of the telly'. She said she had tried everything to encourage him to change but to no avail. I (MN) asked her what kept her trapped in the relationship:

CAROL: Well, he's always saying that if I 'abandon' him – that's the word he likes to use – he'll fall apart and drink himself to death and it will be all my doing.

MICHAEL: Do you agree with that?

CAROL: (*sighs deeply*) Well, yes and no. I can't help feeling that I would be responsible in some way but another part of me says that he's the one in charge of his life, not me, so I should pack up and leave.

MICHAEL: But as you don't pack up and leave, does that mean you remain convinced that it would be your fault if he drank himself to death?

CAROL: I suppose I do feel much more strongly it would be my fault rather than his. It's this guilt that he makes me feel that keeps me trapped. He says that if I walk out on him I'll make him worthless and his life won't be worth living.

MICHAEL: And again, do you agree with that?

CAROL: Hmm. Well, he's not going to think like that unless I leave him, is he? Also his parents would blame me if anything happened to him. They've called me 'selfish' for thinking about leaving him.

MICHAEL: So you would make him think these thoughts about himself if you left and he makes you feel guilty if you left. On top of all this, his parents point the finger at you as well.

CAROL: And before you ask me . . . yes, part of me does think I'm selfish. It's a big mess, isn't it?

MICHAEL: Let's sort it out then. For a start, shall we take a closer look at this issue of who is actually responsible for thinking this or feeling that? You might be surprised with what we come up with.

CAROL: Okay, if it will help me to get away from him.

On the whiteboard in my office, I demonstrated the ABC model of emotional disturbance as it related to Carol's guilt:

A = activating event – imagining her partner's rapid decline and death after her departure

B = beliefs and thoughts – 'I shouldn't have left him but as I did, it's my fault that he died. I'm a terrible person for killing him'

C = consequences (emotional) – intense guilt

Carol was shown that her guilt (C) was largely self-induced, i.e. the principle of emotional responsibility, by her beliefs and thoughts (B) about the consequences of leaving her partner (A) – in the dynamics of guilt, an act of commission that would bring harm to another. Both the act and the self are condemned by the individual.

The principle of emotional responsibility applied equally to Carol's partner. Her departure may have triggered potentially self-destructive thoughts and feelings in him but these were owned by him, not 'put there' by her. This disputing (D) or questioning of her guilt-producing ideas and apportioning of responsibility in the relationship provided the breakthrough for Carol: if she had the 'power' to destroy him through her departure, why did she not have the same power to revive the relationship or make him behave differently? 'Obviously looking at it now in a more objective way, I don't have this power over him and he doesn't have the power to make me feel guilty unless I let him, which I'm not going to do any more.' Through developing an effective (E) guilt-removing outlook, she was now able to move closer to the final step of leaving:

CAROL: I feel apprehensive about telling him because he'll get angry, then he'll feel sorry for himself, then the usual threats about drinking himself to death. Then he'll say he will really change this time. He usually gets on the phone to his parents and they come round to persuade me to give him another chance. After all that pressure, I always gave in. This time I don't want to give in and I certainly don't want to sneak out of the relationship like a thief in the night.

MICHAEL: Well, I can teach you some skills in assertiveness in order to handle this pressure and carry through the decision that you've made.

The principal behavioural method employed was role play where I played the partner and engaged in emotional blackmail to try and change Carol's decision. Initially, she became angry and hurled insults at her 'partner' for past and present hurts; at other times, she became tearful while giving her 'leaving speech' (as she called it). She said she wanted to present her leaving speech 'in a calm, firm and controlled manner and leave with my head held high': 'This relationship ended some years ago for me but I was unable to leave because I allowed myself to be trapped by your emotional blackmail. This is no longer the case and I will be leaving in the morning.'

The sessions were audiotaped so Carol could monitor her verbal performance and a full-length mirror was used so she could practise making her verbal and non-verbal behaviour congruent (videotaping would be even better for this exercise). After several sessions of rehearsing her new behaviour, she delivered her leaving speech to her partner – his parents were also there – and left the relationship. The last session of coaching emphasized maintaining her coaching gains and generalizing assertiveness to other areas of her life where it was indicated.

Follow-up coaching sessions were arranged for three, six and twelve months to monitor Carol's progress. At the three-month follow-up, she said that 'leaving him has really changed my life for the better in so many ways'. Though she expressed no ill-will towards her former partner, she had no interest in or curiosity about his current whereabouts or well-being: 'There's no point in him being out of my life physically if I still let him live with me mentally.'

CONCLUSION

As we have shown in this chapter, assertiveness is not always easy to teach as you can have emotional blocks that prevent or hinder the learning and application of behavioural skills; also, you may harbour misconceptions about becoming assertive that promise more than can be delivered. When misconceptions have been corrected, blocks removed and skills learnt, the act of assertion allows you to make a stand when it matters – 'that is, when they [or you] are too often called upon to deny their true feelings or to bear more than their fair share of the emotional costs of living in harmony with other people' (Sheldon, 1995: 210).

Chapter 8

Taking risks and making decisions

INTRODUCTION

Do you sometimes wish that your life was more exciting and challenging? Yet when such opportunities arise you decide not to grab them because the risk of your decision backfiring is, in your mind, too horrible to contemplate. Therefore, your watchword is 'better safe than sorry' but your yearnings do not disappear: a continual tension exists between being cautious and wishing to take chances. A risk-averse outlook keeps you disgruntled as you accumulate a lifetime of 'if only . . .' regrets (e.g. 'If only I had asked her out when I had the chance but I lost my nerve'; 'If only I had gone on that training course, I could have been higher up the company ladder by now. I didn't want to take the risk of failing the course'). In an echo of Socrates' famous remark that an unexamined life is not worth living, Hauck states that 'the life that has no risk in it is not worth living' (1982b: 57).

We view risk-taking as a sign of psychological health because you want to pursue ambitious goals, are not afraid of setbacks and failures, and want to make your life less self-restricting and more adventurous. However, it is important to stress that we are not advocating that risk-taking *per se* is always good for you, but that each risk you take is carefully considered, not recklessly engaged in (e.g. you drive your car very fast to impress your partner with your 'coolness at the wheel'; she is terrified, says she could have been killed and immediately dumps you). In this chapter, we will examine why you might see risk-taking as something to be avoided or minimized and decision-making as difficult (even though you take risks and make decisions [e.g. motorway driving] every day of your life and these do not present obvious problems for you).

'I CAN'T TAKE THE RISK'

Risk refers to the chance or possibility of an undesirable outcome occurring. The probability of such an outcome 'ranges from practically zero to practically 100 percent' (Wessler and Wessler, 1980: 136). The more feared the outcome, the more probable it is in your mind that it will occur. When you say you cannot take the risk, what you usually mean is: 'I can take the risk but I choose not to' and you 'choose not to' because you believe you will not be able to cope with the consequences of, for example, being rejected or failing. Failure and rejection are probably the two main reasons why people avoid taking risks. Simon would not take the risk of asking Mandy out because she might say 'no' and he believed he would be devastated by her decision. Maxine wanted to leave the NHS and set up in private practice as a therapist but could not accept the risk of 'leaving the nest' and crashing to earth as a failure.

Both Simon and Maxine made the mistake of seeing risk as one-sided (i.e. that the feared calamity would occur) rather than also allowing for the possibility that their desires might be fulfilled; in other words, they assumed their negative predictions were accurate. Also, they saw risk as an outcome fixed in aspic (e.g. forever crushed by rejection; a lifelong failure) rather than as a continuous process of change, adaptation and learning. As Dryden and Gordon observe:

> Life is neither Utopia nor misery because life isn't static. We cannot halt the flow of change. Change is the only continuity you will ever experience so long as you are alive. But the great plus point is that change brings with it the continuing opportunity to modify and shape change. And through accepting that we are both the products and agents of change in an uncertain world, we are offered the possibility of achieving real personal growth. (1993a: 40–41)

Achieving real personal growth can start with you learning to take the 'horror' (emotional disturbance) out of risk-taking: if you think, for example, that rejection or making a mistake is the ultimate horror, how would you evaluate becoming paralysed from the waist down or being horribly disfigured in a fire? If you saw rejection as no more than an inconvenience, you could keep asking women out, accepting rejection and persisting until you got a 'yes'. Of course, you may fear a positive outcome (e.g. receiving a 'yes' means putting in a lot of effort to sustain the relationship; getting the promotion means having to prove to the company that you are worthy of their choice) because you are usually looking beyond the positive outcome to see subsequent failure (e.g. being demoted).

If you do not take risks, then you will have little chance of overcoming your fears or the dull routine of daily life. Risk-taking means that you will have some chance of success on some occasions while avoiding risk means hardly any chance at all of success unless it falls into your lap. In our coaching sessions we encourage people to carry out risk-taking exercises (Neenan and Dryden, 2000; Wessler and Wessler, 1980). These exercises involve people facing their fears and re-evaluating the outcome (e.g. bearable rather than unbearable; unpleasant but not catastrophic). As Walen *et al.* point out:

> People learn by experience: if they have never experienced failure, they will be unlikely to change their IB's [irrational beliefs] about it and their avoidance of it. Thus, it is difficult to work on the fear of an aversive event unless the client actually experiences it. (1992: 265)

Frank described himself as a perfectionist. He dreaded making mistakes in those areas of his life where he believed his credibility was at stake such as public speaking ('If I don't perform perfectly, then people will see me as a phoney'). I (MN) asked him what would happen if he said 'I don't know' to a question he actually knew the answer to:

FRANK: Why would I do something stupid like that?
MICHAEL: To test out your catastrophic prediction that you would be seen as a phoney.
FRANK: Yes, I can see that but I do feel so strongly that it would be the case.
MICHAEL: Your feelings are not facts: you feel it would be the case therefore you assume it's true. What you need to do, if you agree, is to gather accurate information about the outcome and that can only be achieved by taking the risk. What benefits might you gain from this exercise?

FRANK: (*sighs*) I know logically that not being able to answer a question or two is not going to make me a phoney – I don't know anyone who knows their subject one hundred per cent – and I suppose I need to prove this to myself, don't I? The pressure I put myself under is often intolerable.

MICHAEL: In what way?

FRANK: Well, I really drive myself incredibly hard to prepare for these presentations, not to mention how irritable I become with everyone; after the presentation, I'm completely drained and I take several days to recover. So easing the pressure would be another benefit.

MICHAEL: But at the moment these benefits are theoretical because . . .?

FRANK: . . . because I haven't done it yet. (*long pause, then sighs*) I'll reluctantly give it a go then.

When Frank made the momentous confession 'I don't know', there were no shock waves from the audience; instead the question was answered for him by someone in the audience ('He actually made a good point which I would have overlooked'). Evaluations of his presentation were hardly different from previous ones. Frank eventually learnt to be relaxed, but not complacent, about making mistakes while maintaining high (but no longer unrealistically high) standards and that to be revealed as a phoney would have to mean something much more serious than the failure to answer a question ('If someone in the audience had thought I was a phoney because I couldn't answer a question, then he or she has probably got the same attitudes I used to have,' he said at our last session).

Frank was an example of the stress pattern of perfectionism: people 'who desperately demand success but who put so much pressure on themselves for ideal performances that they worry themselves sick as they prepare to act and then experience extreme anxiety while performing' (Bernard, 1986: 206). A second pattern associated with perfectionism is 'giving up', i.e. if you cannot do something perfectly, then you avoid doing it; in this way, by not risking failure, you protect your self-esteem (Bernard, 1986). Instead of aiming high to achieve your cherished goals, you aim low and settle for second best and safety. You may rationalize to your friends and colleagues why you are wasting your talents (e.g. 'I've seen so many people achieve great success and then burn out. I'm not going to put myself through that'). However, the relief from not taking risks and incurring possible failure is usually out-weighed in the longer term by the painful and enduring disappoint-ment of unfulfilled promise.

'I'M NOT CONFIDENT ENOUGH TO TRY IT'

Does confidence come before or after carrying out a difficult activity? You might reply that the logical answer is 'after'. Yet when you are faced with a difficult or uncomfortable task, you may illogically believe that you should feel confident *before* undertaking it and as the feeling remains elusive, you avoid doing the task (were you confident about taking your first driving lesson; if the answer is probably 'no', why did you persist with it?) Avoidance does not develop confidence. In order to feel confident eventually, you need to start off feeling unconfident as you attempt the activity (e.g. learning to dance), acknowledge and analyse your mistakes (e.g. mis-steps), put your new learning into practice, further analysis and practice . . . and so on until you develop performance confidence. In other words, do not put the cart before the horse.

DECISION-MAKING

In this section, our focus is on what you might call unhurried decisions and not on those which involve a rapid response (e.g. working on the stock market) or require split-second timing (e.g. from a racing driver or fighter pilot) which are outside the scope of this chapter.

Decisions, decisions, decisions

Before making a final decision, there are a number of other decisions to consider first. Some examples. How reliable and up-to-date is the information you are going to base your decision on? How do you rate the abilities of the person who is helping you to gather and assess the quality of the information? With regard to yourself, are you placing too much emphasis on the first opinions you listened to (primacy effect) or unduly swayed by what the last person told you (recency effect)? And if you want an objective observer like a trusted friend or colleague to comment on your proposed decision, do you really want to hear an honest appraisal or hoped-for reassurance that you are making the right decision? You may have a plethora of options to choose from, so which ones do you rule out leaving the essential two or three? If your final decision does backfire, do you have another plan of action or are you just praying it turns out successfully?

With so many issues to consider, it may be easy to get bogged down in the technicalities of decision-making and forget the overall purpose of arriving at a decision – to improve your life in some way. So set yourself a realistic timescale for making the decision, estimate the probability of a successful outcome (e.g. 70 per cent) and then make and carry out the decision. If the decision does turn out successfully, further decisions will need to be made by you to maintain that success and troubleshoot any foreseeable difficulties that may threaten it.

'I wish I was decisive'

Decisiveness is usually seen as a positive attribute: for example, people who can think clearly and quickly in a crisis or, once having made a decision, will see it through to the bitter end. From this viewpoint, decisiveness seems to hinge on one crucial decision and a successful outcome will inevitably follow. In reality, decisions need to be made on a moment-by-moment basis in a crisis (and to correct earlier ones) and moving towards the 'bitter end' needs to be regularly reviewed so that it does not become a reality and, instead, just remains a figure of speech. People we see in our coaching sessions who present with difficulties in decision-making are often all-or-nothing thinkers in this area: they see the world as divided into those who are decisive and those who are not (e.g. 'I wish I could be like my colleague, he always knows what to do and doesn't get flustered like me'). We frequently point out that even the most decisive person sometimes vacillates.

On closer examination of their decision-making difficulties, we usually find examples where people have been decisive in their lives (like opting for some coaching sessions) but are currently struggling with certain decisions they have to make. The reasons for their current indecisiveness are then explored. One of us, Dryden (1994c), has listed some self-defeating attitudes underpinning indecisiveness.

1. 'I must be sure that I will make the right decision'

You can only be sure that you have made the right decision by evaluating the outcome of your decision and that can only be achieved by making a decision . . . your thoughts go round and round as if they are on a tape loop. You demand a guarantee before you act yet you know no such guarantee is possible or forthcoming (there is one guarantee: if you continue to demand one, you will remain indecisive). The best you can do is to make a decision based on the available information and have a contingency plan ready if the outcome is a negative one. Right or wrong decisions are based on hindsight, not foresight.

2. 'I must be comfortable when I make decisions'

Choosing between alternative decisions that both contain advantages can leave you feeling uncomfortable as you realize you will not be able to enjoy the advantages of the non-preferred decision. For example, a friend of mine (MN) had two attractive women chasing him and he could not make up his mind which one to go out with as they both excited him; they got fed-up waiting for his decision and eventually lost interest in him. The moral of the story is: it is better to enjoy some advantages than none at all.

Comfort is also a problem when you protest that you cannot make a decision as 'I don't feel right'. If the decision is an especially difficult one (e.g. leaving a relationship) you may actually feel increasingly uncomfortable as you delay making the announcement. If there is any comfort to be experienced, this usually comes after the decision is made, not before it (e.g. 'I'm really glad that's over with and I can now think about something else').

3. 'I must make the right decision because if I make the wrong one, this proves I am stupid and inadequate'

With this attitude, you put your self-esteem on the line when you make a decision. Even if you make a wrong decision, this is hardly conclusive evidence that you are a stupid or inadequate person. If you are making a series of wrong decisions, this points to poor decision-making skills and urgent attention is obviously required.

As we have pointed out elsewhere in this book, your actions can never describe, define or label you because of your complexity as a fallible human being. If you were truly stupid and inadequate, then every decision you made or anything else you ever did in life could only turn out to be inadequate. This reading of human behaviour suggests you cannot learn from your mistakes or change.

4. 'I must make the right decision in order not to lose your approval'

Ellis (1972) suggests that the need for approval lies at the heart of indecisiveness, particularly where tough decisions are called for. For example, Peter's business had run into financial trouble and one of his three employees would have to be dismissed in order to cut back on costs. However, Peter liked his employees and agonized over who it should be ('Whichever one I get rid of will end up hating me and that will bother me a great deal') while the financial costs continued to mount. Peter's decision was eventually made for him as one of them left to seek opportunities elsewhere. Peter's bottom line was the need for approval instead of cutting costs to save his business (Peter said he might have even let his business go to the wall rather than dismiss one of his employees). While the approval of others is desirable, it is not essential to have it and developing a tough-minded attitude (e.g. 'If he doesn't like me, so be it. I can't allow my business decisions to be based on my poll ratings with the staff') will help you become more decisive about unpopular decisions you have to make.

Overdecisiveness

Overdecisiveness usually stems from impulsive decision-making – you act on the spur of the moment instead of thinking through the implications of your decision, and often end up sabotaging your own future interests (e.g. you lose all your savings on Internet trading in stocks and shares because your friend told you how easy it was to make some 'easy money'). Impulsive decision-making is often motivated by how you are feeling at that moment, e.g. you feel down in the dumps and decide to go on a spending spree to cheer yourself up, thereby adding another thousand pounds to your credit card; you feel angry with your boss for cancelling another meeting with you, hurl some abuse at her which leads you to be disciplined.

We would suggest that a lot of impulsive decision-making is fuelled by low frustration tolerance, i.e. you believe you cannot stand the acute discomfort of having to wait, hold your tongue, delay your pleasures or think things through in a methodical fashion. You may defend your impulsive decision-making style as, for example, 'he who hesitates is lost' or 'never pull your punches', but this outlook brings you more poor results than successful ones. Justified caution and pulling punches can rein in your impulsiveness and lead to less rash and more considered decision-making.

Decision-making styles

People obviously differ in their decision-making styles (e.g. cautious vs impulsive) and adopt different styles in different situations. Arnold *et al.* (1995: 257) list six decision-making styles derived from Arroba (1978):

1 No thought
2 Compliant
3 Logical
4 Emotional
5 Intuitive
6 Hesitant

You might be be logical when it comes to work-based decisions (e.g. 'We have four options to carefully consider before presenting our decision to the board') intuitive in judging people (e.g. 'I always go on first impressions, what my gut instinct tells me'), compliant with your partner (e.g. 'If that's what's going to make you happy, then let's do it') and emotional with your children (e.g. 'I like my children to be happy so it's hard for me to say "no" to them'), hesitant about a fitness programme (e.g. 'I don't know if this is for me: I've got to give up cigarettes, cut down on the booze and fry-ups and will I really be any happier?'), and apply 'no thought' to unimportant decisions (e.g. 'Look, I don't care what wine we have with the dinner, so long as it's wet and in a glass').

Some decision-making styles may prove to have more disadvantages than advantages and a change may be required, e.g. more of your decisions regarding your children's behaviour are logical such as 'What lessons am I teaching them and myself if I am reluctant to say "no" to them on some occasions?' rather than emotional as you want to avoid them growing up as 'spoiled brats'.

As well as style, your decisions can be influenced by, among other factors, illness, your emotional state and the amount of stress you are under. With regard to stress, faulty decision-making can occur if you have too little stimulation or stress and for that reason you can be inattentive and not alert when making a decision; or you may be under great pressure and struggling to cope with it and, consequently, do not carefully appraise the various options with the rigour they require (Quick *et al.*, 1997). Therefore, postpone important decisions if you are psychologically off-balance and look for ways to restore the balance (e.g. going for a long walk, putting on the answerphone and enjoying some quiet time, having a swim at lunchtime) so your eventual decision will have less chance of rebounding upon you.

Cost–benefit approach to decision-making
(Dryden, 1994c)

Once you have tackled successfully some of the self-defeating attitudes underpinning poor decision-making, you can then use the cost–benefit analysis forms (see Figure 8.1). There are six steps you need to follow in using these forms (which would be the same steps if you had more than two options).

1.   Describe clearly the two options (A + B) you are going to choose between. Write the option down on each sheet of the cost–benefit form.

2.   Take one of the options (e.g. option A) and focus on the advantages/benefits of choosing this option, both in the short term and in the long term, for yourself and for other people.

3.   Write down the corresponding disadvantages and costs of choosing this option, again in the short term and in the long term, for yourself and for others.

4   Repeat the advantages/disadvantages analysis for the other option (B).

5   Go away for an hour or two and clear your head before coming back to the forms and reviewing what you have written. Read your

Advantages/Benefits of Option A

SHORT TERM

For yourself	For other people
1	1
2	2
3	3
4	4
5	5
6	6

LONG TERM

For yourself	For other people
1	1
2	2
3	3
4	4
5	5
6	6

Disadvantages/Costs of Option A

SHORT TERM

For yourself	For other people
1	1
2	2
3	3
4	4
5	5
6	6

LONG TERM

For yourself	For other people
1	1
2	2
3	3
4	4
5	5
6	6

Figure 8.1   Cost–benefit analysis.

Advantages/Benefits of Option B

SHORT TERM

For yourself   For other people

1	1
2	2
3	3
4	4
5	5
6	6

LONG TERM

For yourself   For other people

1	1
2	2
3	3
4	4
5	5
6	6

Disadvantages/Costs of Option B

SHORT TERM

For yourself   For other people

1	1
2	2
3	3
4	4
5	5
6	6

LONG TERM

For yourself   For other people

1	1
2	2
3	3
4	4
5	5
6	6

Figure 8.1   (continued)

responses on each page and ask yourself the following question: On balance, and taking everything into account, is it better to choose option A or option B? Alternatively (or additionally), you could imagine as vividly as possible what your life might be like (e.g. three, six or twelve months from now) if you chose option A and then do the same for option B. This time-projection procedure (McMullin, 1986) can help you to look back at the present less daunted by the decision you are going to make.

6   Make your decision without any further debate. Even if it is very close, go for the option which overall has the slight edge. Make a commitment to implement it, and then implement it. Even if you make a wrong decision, you will often be happier in the longer term because at least you made the effort and can learn from your experience which will inform your next decision. Endless rumination (e.g. 'Should it be A or should it be B? I don't know. What if I choose A and everything goes wrong? My life will be a mess') only prolongs the agony of indecision.

CREATIVITY

Furnham states that 'Decision making is both a creative and an analytical task' (1996: 36). We have already discussed ways of carefully and critically evaluating alternatives before arriving at a decision. Creativity, on the other hand, involves

> a process called divergent thinking. This involves taking risks with your thinking in ways that may defy logic, appear absurd and seem foolish to other people. As such, creative thinking frequently involves the temporary suspension of critical thinking to enable new ideas to develop, new associations to form and new perspectives to emerge in your mind. (Dryden, 1994c: 61)

In this section, we look at what blocks you from thinking creatively, developing new ideas and implementing them.

'What will people think of me?'

This is a major obstacle to thinking and acting in unfamiliar ways as you overvalue the opinions others hold of you (e.g. 'My friends will think I'm a crank if I tell them I want to try and design a new toothbrush. They're a pretty level-headed bunch so I expect they'll be right'). You stifle your creativity (even if the toothbrush design never gets to the production stage) because you might be frowned upon, condemned or even rejected. Even when wild and spontaneous thinking is actively encouraged such as at brainstorming sessions (i.e. letting your imagination rip in order to generate, for example, many ideas for a new advertising jingle), some members of a brainstorming group will still hold back or only present 'safe' ideas because they fear their contribution will be evaluated negatively and they will be revealed as a fool (Arnold *et al.*, 1995; Furnham, 1996).

What is the worse thing that will happen to you if people mock you? Feeling very uncomfortable? Or receiving confirmation of your own doubts? We would suggest that you tolerate feeling uncomfortable as you try something new, that you have nothing to learn or value from people who are only interested in putting you down, and that it is natural to have doubts about breaking the bounds of conventional behaviour without letting these doubts inhibit you from doing so. As Hauck says: 'Psychological slaves have chains on their brains, not on their legs. You break them by risking more pain. The risk is often worth the subsequent gain' (1981b: 70–71).

Creative suppression (Knaus, 1998)

You may believe that you have some creative talent and would like to write a book, compose music or paint a picture. You have made some occasional attempts to get your creative juices flowing but these usually prove fruitless, reinforcing your doubts about your creative abilities (e.g. 'Why don't I just admit it: I haven't got the talent'). What holds you back from persisting with your artistic endeavours? Sharon highlighted a common problem which I (MN) discussed with her.

SHARON: I'm waiting for inspiration to come and then it will all flow – the book will suddenly all come together. I know that's silly and clichéd – crap really.

MICHAEL: And what do you do with your time while waiting for the inspiration to come?

SHARON: Not much. Waste it on unimportant activities and then get frustrated because I'm not getting on with the book. I feel like giving up sometimes.

MICHAEL: But have you really started yet?

SHARON: What do you mean by that?

MICHAEL: Well, work on your book whether or not you are inspired. How do you know you won't produce some good work even though you start off in an uninspired state?

SHARON: I don't know because I don't try.

MICHAEL: Exactly. So persist with it despite feeling anxious and frustrated that nothing will emerge on that day or in that week.

SHARON: You mean just slog away at it and stop all this nonsense that I can't be creative unless I'm inspired.

MICHAEL: Right. Don't slouch around the house all day wailing 'Muse, where art thou?' Develop a robust outlook: creativity plus persistent effort may eventually realize your ambition of having a book published.

SHARON: I know that's right – some of my favourite writers speak of their daily work schedules . . . but they can say that because they're successful, can't they?

MICHAEL: But how did they get to be and stay successful?

SHARON: Okay, I'm still trying to avoid that uninspired hard slog.

MICHAEL: Do you want to spend the rest of your life torturing yourself as an author manqué?

SHARON: I know people like that who always wanted to be actors or painters but wouldn't take the risk of not making it or being exposed as talentless. I don't want to go down that route.

MICHAEL: Then work your socks off to get your book published and that won't come till you've written it and that won't happen until you invest your time and energy in something you really, greatly want – stop dithering, be determined.

SHARON: I think my slogan will be: 'Be determined, not defeatist.'

Creativity is not something that is usually on tap (e.g. 'I've got a spare hour so I'll knock out another chapter') but you are more likely to have more creative periods if you 'force' yourself to be creative and thereby avoid what Knaus calls 'the eternal plight' of the frustrated artist: 'waiting for moments of inspiration while suffering from a lack of accomplishment' (1998: 153).

'I'm not creative'

In the above example, Sharon believed she had some talent but was not organizing herself or her time in order to try and fulfil that talent. With this block, you genuinely believe that you are not creative, so you convince yourself not to make an ass of yourself trying to be. Like being decisive, you assume that you are either creative or not creative, rather than allowing for some degree of creativity. The first question to ask is: have you really applied yourself to some activity in order to determine if you have creative potential (e.g. creating more exotic menus rather than the standard fare you serve up, or trying your hand at landscape gardening to transform the view from your kitchen window)?

In addition to making a fool of yourself, you may baulk at the discomfort and strangeness involved in stepping outside of your established boundaries and determining 'to boldly go where you haven't been before'. While you may pleasantly surprise yourself by revealing your unexpected creative side (e.g. the local paper publishes some of your poetry) you will also need to tolerate this discomfort and strangeness until it seems less alien to you as you become more familiar with your emerging artistic side.

Another block may be your belief that you have to be intelligent to be creative (e.g. 'I'm not an arty-farty sort of person. I never went to university or anything like that; in fact, I left school without any qualifications'). As Butler and McManus point out, 'Creativity . . . is only weakly correlated with intelligence. Characteristics such as nonconformity, confidence, curiosity, and persistence are at least as important as intelligence in determining creativity' (2000: 50). Taking the risk of venturing into uncharted territory (e.g. 'I fancy having a bash at pottery') will at least give you some idea of your creative potential, while worrying about if you have the 'brains for it' will not.

Some of the people we see in coaching have sought professional help before for their difficulties or have expended a lot of effort trying to resolve them but without much success. Such individuals often state as their goal for change what clearly has not worked previously (e.g. 'I want to find a way to ensure that people always think well of me'). We ask: 'Why reproduce in coaching a failed strategy?' The usual reply is 'I don't know' or 'What else can I do?' accompanied by a shrug of the shoulders. While it might be tempting for us to suggest possible solutions, it is actually counterproductive because this will stifle the person's 'creative efforts to construct new possibilities' (Mooney and Padesky, 2000: 153). Through Socratic questioning (i.e. asking a series of questions to promote insight, better problem-solving and decision-making) the person's creative efforts can be aroused:

MICHAEL: Have you found a way after all these years to ensure that people always think well of you?

SUSAN: No.

MICHAEL: Do you think you will ultimately stumble across the answer?

SUSAN: Probably not. What else am I supposed to do?

MICHAEL: How, ideally speaking, would you like to see yourself?

SUSAN: (*ponders*) As more confident I suppose.

MICHAEL: What might it take to achieve that?

SUSAN: I haven't got the foggiest idea.

MICHAEL: Are there people you particularly like or admire who are the way you want to be?

SUSAN: A couple of people at work and a good friend of mine, Janice; in fact, I wonder what her secret is.

MICHAEL: Why don't you ask her?

SUSAN: Yeah, I could do that. Am I supposed to model myself on her?

MICHAEL: Well, if she reveals what her secret is, what could you do then?

SUSAN: Start trying things out and see what I can learn.

MICHAEL: In order to be Janice Mark Two or a new and improved Susan?

SUSAN: I'd rather be a new and improved Susan.

MICHAEL: So what's the first step in this process of transformation?

SUSAN: (*smiling*) Talk to Janice.

MICHAEL: Good.

Through talking to Janice, Susan said she obtained a valuable piece of advice: 'Why don't you learn to think well of yourself instead of worrying about and wasting time on what others think of you.' In order to discover what 'thinking well of myself' actually meant, Susan acted in an 'as if' capacity, i.e. behaving as if she did think well of herself even if she did not completely believe it (e.g. expressing opinions that might incur others' disapproval, giving herself rewards, planning more activities in her life that were designed to please her rather than to please others, learning to say 'no', becoming less inclined to associate with people who were not friendly towards her). Acting 'as if' was the creative inspiration for

Susan to develop new possibilities for herself and 'give me a view of myself that I didn't think I was capable of'. As Kleinke says:

> There is plenty of psychological research to document a fact we all know from our own experience.
>
> If you want to be,
> Act as if you are,
> And you will become. (1991: 89)

CONCLUSION

Change involves risk. Risk-taking enables you to develop confidence, self-acceptance in the face of setbacks, learning from mistakes and the chance of achieving important goals. Risk-taking is held back by indecision or made unnecessarily perilous by impulsive decision-making. The potential risks and gains of a particular course of action need to be considered carefully. Decision-making also involves being creative, which invites you to suspend temporarily your critical faculties while you let your imagination soar. Once back on earth, you can evaluate these new ideas in terms of their usefulness in helping you to overcome blocks to change and fostering new ways of thinking and acting.

Chapter 9

Understanding the personal change process

INTRODUCTION

Nothing is constant. Change occurs whether you welcome it or fight against it. You cannot be bypassed by change – you are ineluctably caught up in it. You have only to examine your life in the previous six or twelve months to see changes, maybe small and subtle or big and spectacular, some things improving, others possibly deteriorating, and you do not have to be clairvoyant to see that the same process lies ahead of you. The important point is how to make the process of change work beneficially for you (e.g. improved well-being) rather than counterproductively (e.g. increase in personal distress). For example, Derek was made redundant but quickly made plans to retrain, while his friend, Tony, would not accept this reality, wanted his old job back and eventually slipped into depression. In this chapter, we examine what is involved in understanding and negotiating the process of personal change by describing a number of stages to go through.

STAGE 1: ADMIT THAT YOU HAVE A PROBLEM AND TAKE RESPONSIBILITY FOR IT

Before admitting to a problem, you have to be aware that you have one. Others may be aware of it, pointing out changes in your mood and behaviour (e.g. increasingly preoccupied, keeping friends at a distance), but you deny that anything is wrong. Awareness that something is wrong may gradually dawn on you when you notice how uncomfortable or out-of-sorts you feel; problems are piling up which you cannot avoid or a crisis erupts (e.g. your partner threatens to leave if you do not sort yourself out), which forces you to the conclusion that all is not well in your life.

Admitting that you have a problem (e.g. you are having trouble coping with workplace pressures, your drinking is getting out of control or you have sexual difficulties) may become a problem. One of the biggest blocks to admitting to personal difficulties is a feeling of shame: you are revealing to others, or they have found out about, what you perceive to be a weakness, inadequacy or defect, and they will criticize, reject, condemn or mock you for it (e.g. your friends find out about your sexual impotence and make jokes: 'We were right about him after all – he really is a limp dick!'). As Gilbert observes: 'Of all the emotions that are likely to reduce our ability to be helped, to reach out to others and to treat ourselves with compassion, shame is the most important and destructive' (1997: 174). In order to avoid experiencing shameful feelings, you may deny you have a problem, try to cover it up or blame it on others (e.g. 'You make me lose my temper with all your constant nagging'). A very important aspect of admitting to a problem is to accept yourself for having it, irrespective of how others may judge you.

Admitting to a problem means taking responsibility for your thoughts, feelings and actions without blaming yourself, others, society or fate for them (e.g. 'These angry outbursts are my doing and not your fault even though I blamed you for them in the past'). Taking responsibility means that the days of excuses and rationalizations are over with and you are now focused on regaining control over yourself and your life.

STAGE 2: BE SPECIFIC ABOUT YOUR PROBLEM

You will probably find it hard to solve a problem if you discuss it in vague terms (e.g. 'It's something about relationships'). In order to make the problem clear, be as specific as you can about it as demonstrated in this coaching session I (MN) conducted with Alison:

MICHAEL: We need to find out what the 'something' refers to. Does it occur in all relationships or just particular ones?

ALISON: It's really with my husband's friends. I feel uneasy around them.

MICHAEL: What are you uneasy about in their company?

ALISON: Well, like my husband, they've all been to university and they're intelligent, sophisticated and cultured.

MICHAEL: And if they are . . .?

ALISON: I just feel uncultured around them, like I'm a bit of a philistine really. I think that's the problem.

STAGE 3: IDENTIFY YOUR TROUBLESOME EMOTION

We discussed troublesome emotions (i.e. anxiety, depression, guilt, shame, anger, hurt, jealousy, envy) in Chapter 1. To recap, these are emotions that re-occur in a number of situations in your life, seem excessive when the situations are viewed objectively by you, and remain unresolved. They are not incapacitating, nor do they greatly diminish the quality of your life. When identifying the emotion, avoid vague descriptions of it such as 'I feel bad' or 'I feel as if things are not right'. Which of the above troublesome emotions does 'bad' and 'things are not right' refer to? Pinpointing the emotion is the starting point for eliciting the thoughts and beliefs lying behind it. Alison said she felt 'uneasy' in her husband's friends' company, so I asked her which emotion this referred to:

ALISON: Which emotion? Well, I feel uncomfortable, on edge.

MICHAEL: Uncomfortable, on edge, uneasy could refer to anxiety, anger, hurt, for example; so it's important to pin it down.

ALISON: Oh, I see. Definitely anxiety. I get butterflies in my stomach hoping I don't say the wrong thing.

STAGE 4: IDENTIFY THE ASPECT OF THE SITUATION THAT YOU ARE MOST TROUBLED ABOUT

Why is this important? Because it goes right to the heart of the problem in a particular situation and thereby avoids dealing with less important or peripheral aspects of the situation. For example, you might be angry about being deserted by your partner, angry that your life is now empty without her, angry that you have to start finding and building another relationship, angry that your trust has been betrayed, and angry that your former partner is spreading malicious rumours about you. Which aspect of the situation are you most angry about? You might say that your trust has been betrayed and you can never trust again or that your life is now empty which is what you have always tried to avoid. When you discover which aspect of the situation you are most troubled about, then you can develop a realistic attitude to help you cope with it constructively. In Stage 3, Alison thought that being a 'philistine' around her husband's 'cultured' friends was the real problem but she was not sure.

MICHAEL: Shall we see if being a 'philistine' is the aspect of the problem you are most anxious about?

ALISON: Okay.

MICHAEL: If your attitude was 'I couldn't care less about being cultured or what you think of me for being a philistine', would you still be anxious?

ALISON: If I really believed that, then, no, I wouldn't be. I'm anxious about being seen by my husband's friends as uncultured. That's the problem.

MICHAEL: Shall we explore what it means to you to be seen like that?

ALISON: Okay. See what happens.

MICHAEL: What does it mean to you to be seen as uncultured by his friends?

[I am teasing out the personal meaning in each of Alison's responses in order to follow them to their logical conclusion. I assume that each response is temporarily true in order to arrive at her core meaning or belief. This process is called the downward arrow technique (Burns, 1981, 1989) and is discussed in Chapter 1.]

ALISON: (*thinking hard*) Hmm. Well, if they see me as uncultured, then he might too.

MICHAEL: And if he does see you as uncultured . . .?

ALISON: Then he might look at me differently, as if I am stupid and a philistine.

MICHAEL: And if he does see you that way?

ALISON: Then he'll leave me for someone intelligent and cultured.

MICHAEL: What does that mean about you if he leaves you for someone like that?

ALISON: (*eyes moistening*) That I'm inferior. That idea has always been lurking somewhere in my head.

[Alison's core belief has been uncovered.]

MICHAEL: Is that what you are most anxious about: if your husband left you for someone cultured and intelligent, then your long-held belief about your inferiority would really be true, confirmed in your mind?

ALISON: (*slowly nodding*) Yes, unfortunately.

STAGE 5: SELECT YOUR GOALS FOR CHANGE

Goals are the desired outcomes or results that you want for yourself. Though goal-selection may seem relatively easy to do, there are a number of difficulties to watch out for. These include:

- Identifying a goal which is outside of your control, such as 'I want my partner to stop taking me for granted'. In this example, you want someone else to change rather than yourself. You have given your partner the power to achieve your goal, and what happens if he is not interested in it? To bring the goal back within your control, you need to ask yourself what you can start doing (e.g. learning to be assertive) in order to bring to your partner's attention your dissatisfactions. Your new approach may then influence him in making constructive changes in his own behaviour towards you.

- Selecting short-term or 'quick fix' goals which do not address the underlying problems. In the above example, you may decide to put up with his behaviour in order 'to let sleeping dogs lie' and thereby avoid rows and uncomfortable silences in the house. The real unarticulated problem might be your anxiety about antagonizing your partner and him eventually leaving you as you fear living alone. If you were able to imagine yourself coping resourcefully with living alone (long-term goal) this might then encourage you to persist in trying to reform your present relationship. Also, if you remove the fear of living alone you will not bring this inhibiting and self-defeating attitude into your next relationship.

- Stating your goal in negative terms such as 'I don't want to keep on feeling unconfident'. How do you want to feel then? Getting rid of something means putting something else in its place otherwise you will be changing in a vacuum. So you might say, 'I want to feel more confident', and then start discovering and implementing what is required of you to reach and maintain this positive goal.

- Selecting unrealistic goals which are outside of your capabilities such as 'I must be competent at all times'. Such a perfectionistic goal denies your human fallibility, and it is likely to cause you considerable distress when not realised and confirm in your mind that you are incompetent. A more realistic goal may be to increase your level of competency in specific areas and establish benchmarks to evaluate your progress.

  Other unrealistic goals may be ones that are inconsequential or too low, established to avoid experiencing failure (Cormier and Cormier, 1985). For example, you may select just getting a 'pass' in your exam rather than striving for higher grades: 'Unfortunately, the result is usually as inconsequential as the goal itself and often feels like a "hollow victory" with no sense of accomplishment' (Cormier and Cormier, 1985: 224). If you want to produce a good performance or even a personal best, then select difficult goals rather than easy ones: 'this follows from the fact that people direct their behaviour towards goal achievement, so that difficult goals produce more effective behaviour than easy ones' (Arnold et al., 1995: 220-221).

- Feeling calm or unmoved in the face of negative life events. This stoical stance may seem initially desirable but presumably your real intention is to tackle constructively such negative events rather than let your world fall around your ears. Being stoical may be appropriate while facing the dentist's drill, but not if you are unemployed and need to get a job to pay the mortgage.

- Stating your goals in general instead of specific terms, e.g. 'I want to feel happier' vs 'I want to lose two stone in weight'.

The general goal is based on vague yearnings while the specific goal is precise and focused and enables you to shape your behaviour (e.g. diet, exercise) to attain it. Also, achieving your target weight is one step closer to feeling happier; adding more specific goals to your list (e.g. going on adventure weekends and singles' holidays) may eventually bring you the general goal that several months earlier seemed just a pipe dream. Breaking a general goal into specific ones provides you with an action plan for change.

- Setting goals that may conflict with your ethical standards. For example, you may believe that trust is the basis of a loving and enduring relationship, but you decide to lie to your partner about the money you lost through gambling in order not to upset her. However, the guilt you feel 'eats away' at you because you are 'living a lie' and the relationship suffers accordingly. In line with your ethical standards, you eventually decide to tell the truth (e.g. 'I feel so much better now'), face the consequences (e.g. your partner feels let down and keeps her distance from you for several days) and promise to stop gambling.

Goals, once decided upon, are not set in concrete and may have to be altered in the light of information gathered from your goal-directed actions. For example, you may decide to reduce gradually to zero your cigarette intake over a month-long period; but after several days you realize you are just 'torturing' yourself with a slow withdrawal programme and decide to stop there and then and 'tough it out' until the cravings eventually disappear.

I now return to a discussion of Alison's goals for change:

MICHAEL: You said that the problem was feeling uneasy, anxious around your husband's friends in case you were revealed as uncultured. When we explored the meaning of being uncultured you came to the conclusion that you were inferior. Okay, so far?

ALISON: Yes, I'm following. So what do I do about it?

MICHAEL: Well, you could ask your husband's friends or even your husband if they or he see you as uncultured.

ALISON: I'm sure they don't. It's just my insecurities.

MICHAEL: So if they didn't see you like that, how would you feel in their company?

ALISON: More relaxed.

MICHAEL: What would happen if you met new friends of your husband?

ALISON: (*ponders*) The anxiety would come back for the same reasons. Back to square one.

MICHAEL: So is asking others if they see you as uncultured the solution to your problems?

ALISON: No, that solution won't last. I'm expecting them to solve my problem, to make me feel better about myself.

MICHAEL: So what solution has more chance of lasting and is within your control?

ALISON: Not seeing myself as inferior. I would like to leave that behind.

MICHAEL: In terms of a goal for change, it is better to be working towards something positive rather than simply saying what you don't want or what you want to leave behind?

ALISON: I could learn to be cultured by going to the ballet, opera, art galleries, that sort of thing.

MICHAEL: Is that because you truly want to do that or gain the approval of others through doing it?

ALISON: (*sighs deeply*) Gain the approval of others – the wrong reasons.

MICHAEL: So how would you like to see yourself on your terms?

ALISON: That I can accept myself, warts and all.

MICHAEL: If you could believe that, how do you think your life would be?

ALISON: Well, I'd just be more relaxed generally, I wouldn't make myself anxious around my husband's friends, I'd feel more confident and not give myself such a hard time. Sounds so simple when I say it like that.

MICHAEL: Any drawbacks to being like that?

ALISON: (*musing*) Any drawbacks? I suppose what effect it might have on my marriage.

MICHAEL: Which might be what?

ALISON: Er . . . I'm not sure. My husband has always said that he married me for me, not whether I visit art galleries or go the opera. I don't know really. Just a vague feeling I suppose.

MICHAEL: If the feeling becomes something more concrete then we can examine it. So do you want to pursue this goal of accepting yourself on your terms?

ALISON: I do. It's about time that I did.

STAGE 6: CHALLENGE AND CHANGE CORE BELIEFS

The three criteria of logic, reality-testing and helpfulness are used to examine core beliefs. We will use the example of failure to demonstrate this examination process.

1. Logic. If you have experienced some failures in your life (e.g. loss of a job, end of a relationship), how does it logically follow that you are a failure as a person? You might reply that it does, but would you condemn your children, partner, friends, in a similar way for their failures? The usual answer we receive is 'No' which then leads to our next question: 'What makes you special that you deserve self-condemnation while you are compassionate and understanding towards others?' The issue to decide for yourself is whether your arguments are sound or illogical and inconsistent. We would argue that the latter is the case and state that you can never be a failure as a person no matter how many times you fail – you have intrinsic worth as a human being irrespective of your successes and failures in life.

2. Reality-testing. Does your belief reflect empirical reality? Your subjective viewpoint is compared with your objective experience: if you are a failure as a person, then all you can ever do is fail at every single thing you attempt. Is that an accurate description of your life? Obviously not because you are successful at some things and fail at others. Weighing evidence dispassionately can help you to make more accurate appraisals of your life as it actually is. When some people tell me (MN) they are failures, I ask them, for example, how they were able to organize themselves successfully in order to get to the coaching session on time. Reality-testing encourages you to act in the role of a personal scientist by viewing your beliefs and ideas as hypotheses instead of as facts. Gathering evidence helps you to confirm or disconfirm your hypotheses.

3. Helpfulness. Does the idea that you are a failure help you to overcome your problems and feel better? This is rarely the case though you might argue that calling yourself a failure may motivate you to do better (we see this as a demotivating strategy as you keep on trying to prove what you are not rather than focusing on achievement and problem-solving based on self-acceptance).

Spelling out the consequences of holding onto the idea that you are a failure can often be the most powerful argument for surrendering it.

Developing self-acceptance

You are neither inferior nor superior as a person for having or not having problems. So what are you then? As we have argued throughout this book, you are a fallible (imperfect) human being who refuses to rate yourself on the basis of your actions or characteristics but does rate those aspects of yourself which you wish to change or improve (e.g. 'I can accept myself for having panic attacks but I really wish I didn't have them; so I will be seeking professional help to overcome them'). Without self-acceptance, you may be continually side-tracked from problem-solving by shame-fuelled self-denigration (e.g. 'I'm weak and pathetic for having panic attacks'). We often demonstrate self-acceptance through the use of the 'big I/little i' diagram (Lazarus, 1977; see Figure 9.1).

Hauck calls the self 'every conceivable thing about you that can be rated' (1991b: 33). The big 'I' stands for the self and the little 'i's represent every conceivable thing about you that can be rated (e.g. having or not having a job or relationship, hair style, height, age, weight, lying to a friend, giving money to charity) – the list is limitless. The mistake is to assume that some of the little 'i's equal the complexity and totality of the self (e.g. 'Because I lied to my friend therefore I'm no good'); you could equally say that giving money to charity makes you a good person. Both descriptions of you would be wholly inaccurate.

You may think this idea is too far-fetched (e.g. 'Of course you're a failure if you make mistakes'), but we would bet that you do not rate your children on the basis of their behaviour (e.g. 'You've been naughty at school. Therefore you are a thoroughly bad little boy and will never change'). So we would advise you not to do it to yourself. In essence, when you concentrate on the big 'I' you are self-focused and likely to be self-attacking, whereas with your attention on the little 'i's you are in a problem-solving and goal-orientated frame of mind (even if the goal is to accept without unduly upsetting yourself what you cannot change).

You may have similar rating tendencies towards your role. For example, as a mother or manager, you could construct a big 'M' containing lots of little 'm's and criticize and improve where

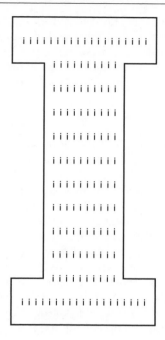

Figure 9.1   The big I/little i diagram.

possible the little 'm's without using them to label the big 'M' (in terms of roles, you could go from A [e.g. actor] to Z [e.g. zoo-keeper]).

If you disagree with the concept of self-acceptance or see it as unattainable, then strive to develop a multidimensional identity (Linville, 1987): 'People who have a one-dimensional view of themselves are very limited. They don't have a broad foundation of personal resources to fall back on when facing difficult challenges' (Kleinke, 1991: 208). For example, if your work is your worth, what will happen to your self-esteem when you lose your job or retire? If your partner is your reason for living, your thoughts might turn to self-harm if he leaves you or dies? Therefore, 'good copers have a life philosophy of developing their personal identity along many dimensions' (Kleinke, 1991: 208). In other words, do not put all your eggs in one basket.

Alison's belief of seeing herself as 'inferior' is examined through using logic, reality-testing and helpfulness:

MICHAEL: In terms of logic, how does it make sense to say that you are inferior as a person because you see yourself as uncultured?

ALISON: I suppose it doesn't make sense but I don't know why.

MICHAEL: Would you call people who are short, or blind, or live in council houses, or left school without any qualifications, inferior people?

ALISON: Of course I wouldn't.

MICHAEL: Why not?

ALISON: Because they can't help being short, blind or living in council houses. Those things about them don't make them inferior.

MICHAEL: What would make them inferior in your eyes?

ALISON: Well . . . er . . . nothing I can think of. They're just people coping with their circumstances. I don't know what else to say.

MICHAEL: If nothing you can think of would make other people inferior, how does being uncultured make you inferior?

ALISON: I don't know but I would usually say that it does. Okay, I don't know but I need to think about it more.

MICHAEL: Okay, let's ask if your belief is realistic: if you were inferior, what evidence would you need to prove it?

ALISON: I suppose other people would treat me as if I were inferior. Some people have been rude to me sometimes.

MICHAEL: Is that evidence of your inferiority or their impoliteness?

ALISON: Their impoliteness.

MICHAEL: Let's focus on this issue of inferiority: if the world or other people truly saw you as inferior, how would you be treated?

ALISON: I suppose I'd be rejected, despised, always pushed to the back of the queue, pointed at, a permanent second-class citizen.

MICHAEL: Is that your actual experience?

ALISON: No, but I sometimes wonder if some people see me as inferior for not having a university degree.

MICHAEL: If some people do see you that way, where's the proof that it makes you inferior?

ALISON: The proof is in here (touching her head) not out there (pointing towards the window). I just believe sometimes that I should be reading Shakespeare instead of the *Sun* and watching ballet rather than the soaps. That's all.

MICHAEL: Even if your cultural preferences are not what you would like them to be or are lacking in balance, this might be an occasion for regret but, again, where is the evidence that you, Alison, are inferior if you don't read Shakespeare or superior if you do?

ALISON: I suppose my bearings are all confused. I've never really thought about the things you're asking me.

MICHAEL: Okay. Let's look at the issue of helpfulness. Where does it get you believing you are inferior?

ALISON: Nowhere. Just worried sometimes that I might be exposed as an ignoramus when asked my views on a new play that I've seen or something like that. I can't think of any good that it does me.

MICHAEL: If that's the case, why do you stick with a belief that does you no favours?

ALISON: (*long pause*) Well, I suppose seeing myself as inferior niggles away at me to improve my mind and eventually have a higher opinion of myself.

MICHAEL: And how far away are you from that higher opinion of yourself?

ALISON: About a million miles.

MICHAEL: We have had an introductory look at your belief that you are inferior to see if it is logical, realistic and helpful. What happened?

ALISON: My belief failed all three tests but I'm not convinced yet. So what's next then?

MICHAEL: Going over these and other arguments again and again until you are able to see that calling yourself inferior is illogical, unrealistic and unhelpful. At the same time, we need to look at developing an alternative self-image based on what you wanted, which was, quote, 'that I can accept myself, warts and all', unquote.

I explained the 'big I/little i' diagram to Alison by circling some of the little 'i's representing aspects of herself (e.g. being uncultured, not going to university, her anxiety) and then judging herself, her totality as a human being – the big 'I' – on the basis of these little 'i's. I asked her about her good points and I circled some more little 'i's (e.g. keeping fit, good cook, doing charity work) and asked her if these good points totally described her complexity as a human being any more accurately than her bad points did? She began to see that that it was illogical to judge herself on the basis of particular actions, characteristics or experiences and that striving to accept herself as a fallible human being could eventually overcome her self-rating as inferior and prevent any further self-rating. Also, as human beings are in a state of flux, little 'i's will disappear from the big 'I' (e.g. giving up smoking, losing your hair) while new ones (e.g. reaching forty years of age, changing careers) will be added. Again, how can your continual life changes be summed up by a single label?

However, Alison was worried that self-acceptance implied complacency and stasis ('I might not bother with anything or push myself if I learn self-acceptance'). I replied that self-acceptance is the basis for personal development and goal-directed behaviour and the avoidance of self-denigration which uses up valuable time and energy and is goal-deflecting. If she worked hard to internalize self-acceptance, then in three, six or twelve months' time, she could assess the benefits of this new way of viewing herself.

STAGE 7: STRENGTHEN YOUR NEW OUTLOOK

In strengthening your new beliefs or self-helping outlook, it is important to think and act in ways that are consistent with it and refrain from thinking and acting in ways that are inconsistent with it. In other words, ensure that your beliefs, thoughts and behaviours are working in concert. For example, if your new outlook is to be open and honest about your gay lifestyle, then your thoughts (e.g. 'No more lies or self-deception. Now it's time to face people and let them see the real me') and behaviours (e.g. taking your partner to meet your parents and friends) need to reflect it. Thoughts (e.g. 'Maybe I haven't tried hard enough to be heterosexual') and behaviours (e.g. not being seen in public with your partner) which militate against internalizing your new outlook need to be challenged in order to weaken their 'hold' on you.

Continual practice in adopting new ways of thinking and behaving may produce a puzzling phenomenon – you do not feel any different (e.g. 'I don't call myself a loser any more, I tackle problems as soon as they appear instead of procrastinating over them, but I still feel miserable. How come?'). The reason for this is because emotional change often lingers behind changes in your thoughts and behaviours and therefore takes time to 'catch up'

(Dryden, 1995). Significant emotional change usually occurs when you have deep conviction in your new outlook; so do not become discouraged when your feelings appear not to budge in the early stages of the change process.

You will not believe in your new ideas until you put them into daily practice in forceful and persistent ways (e.g. staying in situations you previously avoided in order to overcome your panic symptoms). Acting on them occasionally or in a milk-and-water manner will not usually produce much, if any, real change (e.g. 'I've tried to stay in those situations but I feel so uncomfortable and jittery that I have to leave'). Internalizing a new outlook involves a commitment from you 'to doing the work necessary to bring about the changes you want. Without this commitment, your efforts may very well be sporadic and half-hearted, and your gains will be slow, accidental, and incomplete' (Grieger, 1991: 39). So be committed. For example, if you avoid unpleasant or difficult tasks that you know you should be tackling, then immerse yourself in them and work through your disturbed thoughts and feelings (e.g. 'No matter how angry I get about this bloody boring paperwork, I will finish it and any other paperwork that requires my attention now or in the future').

However, your commitment to change and the hard work associated with it may be undermined by what one of us, Dryden (1994c), calls the 'five major traps'.

Trap 1. I cannot take constructive action until I am comfortable

If you believe that only when you feel comfortable will you be able to initiate change, then change will be delayed indefinitely. When you start taking constructive action you will feel uncomfortable at first but as Ellis points out:

> If you push and push and push yourself, as you would have to do at playing the piano or at any sport you want to excel at, you'll *finally* find it easy and enjoyable. Not at first – but *finally*! So *make* yourself do the work you dislike, force yourself to do it and do it. Deliberately *push* yourself to be *un*comfortable – yes, *un*comfortable – until you finally find the work easy and comfortable. (1985: 102; italics in original)

By courting discomfort now you will be able to make yourself comfortable later.

Trap 2. I cannot take constructive action because I do not have a sense of control

A sense of control is gradually established by venturing forth and accepting that you currently feel out of control. For example, mastering your panic symptoms will only come by entering and staying in those situations that trigger your panic attacks until your symptoms subside. Through daily practice of this 'staying-in-there' technique, you gain a sense of control over your panic. If you keep on telling yourself that 'I must be in control' *before* undertaking action, you will only reinforce the idea that you are out of control.

Trap 3. I cannot act differently because I do not feel competent yet

Competence is not usually achieved in one fell swoop. Trial and error is usually the order of the day. So expect to act incompetently, but through learning from your mistakes you will notice a transition from acting incompetently to performing competently. It is highly doubtful that you will be able to bypass this learning process.

Trap 4. I cannot take new action which is strange to me because I do not feel confident to do so

It is perfectly natural to feel unconfident about acting in new and strange ways – how could it be otherwise? Unless you persist in these 'strange' actions and accept that this is the way it should be if you eventually want to become confident, you will probably give up and return to familiar ways that you actually want to change. The more you practice these new actions the quicker they will feel less strange and more natural to you.

Trap 5. I cannot undertake constructive actions, particularly those which are risky for me, because I do not have the courage to do so

People who perform courageous acts do not usually say things like 'I felt deeply courageous and that's why I rescued the child from the burning building'. The more standard reply is that they believed it was the right or necessary action at the time even though they were afraid or highly anxious. Gaining courage in facing your fears comes from action, not waiting around until you feel courageous – the longer you wait for the feeling to arrive the more likely you are to convince yourself that 'I haven't got the guts to take these chances' and settle for second-best and a pattern of avoidance.

With all five traps, there is a paradox at work in personal change: if you want to feel comfortable, be in control, act competently, confidently and courageously, then you first need to feel uncomfortable or out of control, and to act incompetently, unconfidently and uncourageously (Dryden, 1993). So when considering what changes you wish to make in your life, remember that struggle comes first, success later.

Alison's goal was to accept herself, warts and all. She continually challenged her belief that she was inferior by using the three criteria of logic, reality-testing and usefulness. To put into practice the idea of self-acceptance, Alison began to tell her husband's friends that she was not interested in 'cultural pursuits' and that she much preferred watching *EastEnders* or *Coronation Street* and would explain current plotlines to them (previously she would pretend to hang on to every word they said and try to play the 'culture vulture'). In addition, she would let them see her reading the *Sun* when they arrived at the house and chat to them about the 'shocking' revelations of a pop star's sex life (before, she would hide the newspaper). Even though Alison felt very unconfident and uncomfortable in acting this way, she could see the rationale for it:

ALISON: If I don't put it into practice what we've been discussing, then all this self-acceptance stuff is just pie in the sky.
MICHAEL: Exactly. So how are you getting on?
ALISON: Well, sometimes I overdo my real interest in the *Sun* or *EastEnders* in order to get the point across that they can take or leave me, but whatever their reaction is, the important point is for me not to put myself down.
MICHAEL: What has been their response?
ALISON: Apart from a few comments that the *Sun* can seriously damage your mental health, nothing much really. Some people have asked me why I've suddenly started behaving differently.

MICHAEL: What did you reply?

ALISON: I was honest with them about my previous feelings of inferiority and that I'm learning self-acceptance and no longer trying to pretend what I'm not. I can't believe at times that I'm being so open about these things but it's becoming liberating because I'm worrying less what others think about me.

MICHAEL: What's been the general reaction of your husband's friends?

ALISON: Most of them couldn't really care. What I thought would happen – things like them looking down their noses at me, treating me with contempt – didn't happen, so I was really surprised about that. One or two of them though have been a bit snotty about it but I've always thought that they thought my husband married beneath him. Of course, I used to agree with that.

MICHAEL: And now?

ALISON: I don't believe that now but there are days when I start to wobble again and think: 'What does he see in a thicko like me?' But that's to be expected, isn't it?

MICHAEL: Yes, it is. Change doesn't remove all your doubts, just that they inhibit you less.

ALISON: I can see that. Do you know what? Now that I'm thinking about what I really want for myself instead of trying to get the approval of others, I'm actually considering doing a degree through the Open University because now I'm genuinely interested in it. Bizarre, isn't it?

MICHAEL: Good for you.

STAGE 8: GENERALIZE YOUR GAINS TO OTHER RELEVANT SITUATIONS

The gains you make in one situation (e.g. tolerating the intense discomfort of repeatedly asking your next-door neighbour to turn down his loud music) can be extended to other difficult inter-personal contexts such as standing your ground with colleagues who try to dump some of their work on you or saying 'No' to friends who may regard you at times as a taxi service. Do not assume that these gains will automatically transfer to new situations; in fact, you may well have to start from scratch again in tackling a new situation (e.g. 'I now can give as good as I get with my neighbour, so why do I still still walk on eggshells with some of my work colleagues?'). Tolerating discomfort in one context may pose different challenges in another (e.g. 'At least with my neighbour I don't have to live with him but with some of my colleagues there will be a bad atmosphere in the office every day which I'll have to put up with. I don't fancy that'). Generally speaking, if you want your gains to extend to other situations, then undertake an action plan to bring this about.

Accepting herself in the face of her husband's friends' presumed or actual disapproval was Alison's first step. She then stopped putting herself in an intellectually subordinate position with those work colleagues who had university degrees (e.g. 'I always thought "I'm not as smart as them because I haven't been to university"') and started giving her opinions and arguing her corner (this did not mean she had to win every argument or attempt to get people to respect her but to signal to herself and others that she no longer saw herself as inferior). Her greatest apprehension was how her husband would react to her new stance 'even though he has told me time and time again that he accepts me for myself'. Instead of 'tagging along' with her husband to cultural events 'which often bored the living daylights out of me', she began pursuing more of her own interests and therefore spent less time in his company. I asked her how he was reacting to this:

ALISON: He's not bothered. He says it's about time I developed my own interests and thought things through for myself. He's been very supportive.

MICHAEL: Okay, let me jump to the worst outcome. How would you react if your husband didn't approve of your new behaviour or only had accepted you as long as you played the obedient wife and not tried to rise above your intellectual station in life?

ALISON: Before I would have been devastated that he only married me because I was obedient and a thicko, but now . . . (*long pause*) but now, and if that really was the case, I would try to build a different kind of relationship with him or if that fell apart or he didn't agree with it, then I would end up leaving him as very sad as that would be. You know, saying these things to you would have inconceivable just six months ago. I feel for the first time in my life that I'm becoming my own person.

STAGE 9: MAINTAIN YOUR GAINS

Whether you have made progress and achieved your goals through coaching sessions or a self-initiated change programme, it is important to remember that your gains are unlikely to be maintained unless you consistently work to support them (e.g. getting fit is not the same as staying fit – both require sustained effort from you). Even if you work hard to avoid a reactivation of your problems, there is no guarantee that they will disappear for good.

However, in order to minimize the chances of their reappearance, you can list vulnerability factors in your life that might trigger a lapse (stumble) or a relapse (collapse). For example, you might see holiday periods when you are likely to be alone as vulnerable times for you that could lead back to overeating, inactivity and low mood ('When I spend too much time on my own, the old idea that I'm unlikeable tends to sneak back'). For such occasions, you can prepare an action plan that would involve daily activities, people you could phone or group activities such as adventure weekends – anything that would reduce the time spent alone. Eventually, spending time alone rather than avoiding it would need to be faced as part of your coping and self-acceptance strategy – you choose to spend time with yourself rather than seeing yourself being forced into it because 'no one likes me'.

If you do have a lapse, try to avoid condemning yourself for it (e.g. 'I'm weak. I'll never change'). Instead, adopt a problem-solving focus and analyse the factors leading up to it as part of your continuing learning process (e.g. 'I deliberately engineered a row with my wife so I could storm out of the house, go to the nearest pub and start drinking again. I used it as an excuse because I still haven't convinced myself yet that alcohol does more harm than good in my life, but I'm getting there'). In this way you can strive to prevent a lapse turning into a relapse. Even if you have a relapse, you can analyse it in the same way to extract learning from it (e.g. 'This bender only lasted a couple of days. The last time I went off the rails I was drunk for several weeks. That's progress').

Maintaining your gains involves a lifelong commitment to hard work. This initially sounds like a dispiriting message but, from our own experience, we know that the hard work gets easier the more of it you do. So less work now equals more effort later while more work now equals less effort later.

Alison had been working hard to make self-acceptance a daily reality but sometimes found it hard going:

ALISON: Why didn't I know about all this stuff twenty years ago? I should have known. I feel I've wasted so much time in my life dragging this inferiority complex around with me. I wonder if I'm any happier with this new knowledge.

MICHAEL: Okay, let's start with why you didn't know about this stuff twenty years ago. What's the answer to that?

ALISON: I didn't know about self-acceptance. It's as simple as that.

MICHAEL: So why give yourself a hard time by saying that you should have known what you didn't know at the time?

ALISON: I know it's silly but these ideas do cling on.

MICHAEL: Then be more forceful about prising loose their grip. Now, has all the past twenty years been a waste?

ALISON: It feels like it some time but when I'm thinking clearly I know that's not the case. It's been good and bad, up and down. I suppose like most other people's lives.

MICHAEL: If you spend the next twenty years lamenting the waste of the last twenty, what then?

ALISON: (*laughs*) Forty years of waste!

MICHAEL: Did you think that applying this new knowledge would be straightforward rather than an emotional rollercoaster at times?

ALISON: I suppose I did think it would be easier than it is. I keep on questioning things more now than I ever did before in my life.

MICHAEL: That's part of the change process. Things will start to level out when you feel more at home with your new way of being. Are these changes worth persisting with though?

ALISON: Yes. I'm not going to turn back now. I know and hope deep down that what lies ahead of me will be more interesting and exciting than what went before.

Follow-up coaching sessions were arranged for three, six and twelve months' time to monitor her progress.

CONCLUSION

Between desiring change and achieving it, there are a number of stages to pass through. These stages provide structure to the change process and markers for assessing progress (e.g. not taking responsibility for your problem is likely to keep you stranded in Stage 1). Coping successfully with the personal change process requires you to learn from and adapt to its vicissitudes. Such an outlook will stand you in good stead for present and future problem-solving.

Chapter 10

Putting it all together

INTRODUCTION

In the previous chapters, we hope that we have shown you ways of tackling successfully a range of difficulties that will help you to achieve greater personal effectiveness. Definitions of personal effectiveness are, of course, highly subjective, e.g. one person may see being assertive in certain situations as her desired outcome while another wants to develop a time management strategy that maximizes every minute of his waking life. Obviously you will need to determine specific criteria which will tell you if you are indeed achieving your goals, e.g. engaging in boring or burdensome tasks instead of avoiding them, handling criticism without being defensive or aggressive, removing time-wasting activities from your daily work schedule, and developing persistence instead of giving up at the first obstacle.

Your view of personal effectiveness will probably change over time as you develop greater competence and confidence in managing difficulties and responding to challenges, e.g. risk-taking is now seen by you as an indispensable and exciting part of personal growth, whereas before you viewed it apprehensively as containing more dangers than benefits. In this chapter, we focus on what we consider to be the building blocks of increased personal effectiveness.

SELF-ACCEPTANCE

We have discussed this concept repeatedly in this book because we think it is vitally important in developing and maintaining emotional stability in your life. Internalizing a philosophy of self-acceptance helps you to avoid putting yourself down and keeps your focus on your actions, traits and experiences (e.g. 'I made a mess of this situation, which I want to learn from, but I'm not useless because of it'). Self-acceptance greatly reduces the duration, frequency and intensity of your troublesome emotions because you refrain from attacking yourself which is often at the heart of such emotions.

We distinguish self-acceptance from self-esteem: self-acceptance is unconditional – no strings attached – whereas self-esteem is conditional. You may say that you have self-esteem because . . . the word 'because' indicates the provisional nature of your 'self-acceptance' as it is usually linked to positive things in your life such as a job, partner, car, holidays, close friends, etc. or other specified conditions (e.g. having the respect of your colleagues, maintaining high standards). If these things or conditions are absent from your life, it is likely that your self-esteem will be badly shaken or even dissolve (e.g. 'I can't maintain my high standards any more. What's wrong with me? I'm a failure'). The only time *all* the evidence is in about your life and yourself is on your deathbed, so any judgements you make before that time are both premature and inaccurate.

Having said all that, we acknowledge that unconditional self-acceptance is unrealizable because we are imperfect human beings who will on occasions rate our actions and then rate ourselves on the basis of them (e.g. 'I don't really understand what self-acceptance is, so I must be stupid'). Realistically, strive for much greater self-acceptance, thereby keeping to a minimum the times you denigrate or rate yourself.

A fair measure of self-acceptance helps you to be authentic with yourself by honestly acknowledging your true feelings, beliefs and values and trying not to convince yourself that you should be other than you are (though this view in no way prevents you from addressing those aspects of yourself you wish to change). Being authentic with others is important too instead of trying to seek their approval, 'put on faces' for them or hide your weaknesses from them (we are not suggesting that you have to make a full and immediate confession of your failings every time you meet someone new – only selective self-exposure when you deem appropriate).

HIGH FRUSTRATION TOLERANCE

We believe that one of the key blocks to change is low frustration tolerance, i.e. you want to achieve your longer-term goals but 'throw in the towel' when you encounter setbacks, frustrations, discomfort; in other words, you are not prepared to endure the hard and uncomfortable work of change in order to reach your goals. For example, if you want to get out of debt, then it will be necessary to forgo or greatly reduce present pleasures (i.e. keep a tight rein on your financial outgoings) until the debt is paid off. You may see the perfect sense in this but believe it is 'too hard' to give up temporarily your pleasures and thereby sabotage your longer-term goal, i.e. you stay in debt or increase it. By avoiding the hard work of the present, you actually make things harder for yourself in the long run.

Adopting an outlook of high frustration toleration (e.g. 'I don't like all this hard work but I can see why it's necessary, so I'll stick with it') helps you to endure in order to find enduring solutions to problems, avoids defeating your longer-term interests by seeking quick fixes, and encourages you to re-evaluate your ideas that struggle and hard work are unbearable. Reading accounts of how people endure in extreme conditions (e.g. Bettelheim, 1960; De Rosario, 1995; Frankl, 1985) can be inspirational and motivate you to persevere with your own efforts at change.

THINK FOR YOURSELF

You may think that some of your beliefs are the result of brainwashing (e.g. 'Society makes you feel that you're inferior or no good if you're overweight') or 'given' to you by others (e.g. 'My partner says I'm a failure, so he must be right'). In both examples, you are *uncritically* accepting these messages instead of asking yourself: 'What do I really think about what they're saying?' We would argue that if you do believe you are inferior for being overweight or see yourself as a failure that is because *you* have ultimately chosen to believe these things – they have not been 'forced' into your head. For example, if the fashion industry started a campaign which said that being overweight was sexy and glamorous, would you automatically agree with it and, if you were slim, would you deliberately put on weight?

Another obstacle to clear thinking is overgeneralizing about yourself, others and the world (e.g. 'I'm weak', 'Every one is against me' and 'Nothing ever goes right'). Instead, view these things along a continuum (i.e. seeing events in relative rather than absolute terms) which will help you to develop a more accurate and realistic appraisal of them (e.g. 'I have weaknesses and strengths', 'My family and a few friends still support me' and 'Some things go right and some things go wrong'). Try to remain open-minded to alternative viewpoints and new evidence, take nothing for granted, do not be intimidated by the views of others (e.g. experts, gurus, politicians) or prevailing orthodoxies (e.g. political correctness) or agree with what you really do not believe because you seek others' approval and do not want to be the odd one out in a group (the famous experiments carried out by Solomon Asch in the 1950s looked at the difficulties of disagreeing with majority opinion). Thinking clearly and honestly can help you to be more independent-minded.

TAKE CALCULATED RISKS

We emphasize calculated risks, not impulsive or foolish ones. Calculated risks are based on considering the short- and long-term consequences of a particular course of action (e.g. leaving a relationship, becoming self-employed). Risk-taking can create new and exciting possibilities for you (e.g. 'What would I really like to do in my life?') but also, of course, involves failures and setbacks. You may invest a great deal of time and effort in a particular activity which turns out unfavourably; instead of feeling despair, learn from your experiences in order to make better decisions next time. We would suggest that trying and sometimes failing is better than never trying at all.

BALANCE YOUR SHORT- AND LONG-TERM INTERESTS

Living only for the present can undermine your longer-term interests while forgoing all current pleasures for longer-term achievements can make your present life dull and miserable. We suggest that you keep your eye on the present and the future in order to arrive at a balance between competing interests. For example, some partygoing and intensive study can provide present enjoyment but also make you keenly aware of the requirements of your chosen career. Ellis sums up this balance succinctly: 'The seeking of pleasure today and the non-sabotaging of tomorrow's satisfac-tions' (1980: 18).

LEARN TO ACCEPT UNCERTAINTY

We live in a world of probability and chance where no absolute guarantees exist (even death might one day be abolished by medical advances). If you demand certainty of outcome or success before you embark on various activities, you will probably become paralysed with indecision and afflicted by a good deal of emotional torment. Even if someone you trusted guaranteed that you would succeed, would you completely believe her? Probably not, because she might be wrong; so even if you get the guarantees you are demanding, your uncertainty does not disappear. If you accept uncertainty in life (without having to like it), then you realize

> that judgements and decisions can be made with no guarantee that things will work as planned. Mature, effective people make their decisions based on incomplete knowledge, and responsibly cope with the outcomes of their decisions and learn from each one so as to increase their knowledge for future decisions. (Dryden and Matweychuk, 2000: 86)

Instead of endlessly worrying about uncertainties in life, become probabilistic-minded, i.e. think that you will probably get more of what you want from life and less of what you do not want if you work hard, take risks and are determined.

SELF-RESPONSIBILITY

This means that you are ultimately responsible for the way you think, feel and behave no matter what contributed to your present difficulties. For example, you blame your partner's unfaithfulness for making you feel depressed as you believe his behaviour proves you are unattractive, whereas the division of responsibility is actually this: he is responsible for his unfaithfulness and you are responsible for your self-evaluation of being unattractive and, consequently, your depression (e.g. 'If I'm unattractive, he will leave me. What can I do to make him desire me again and stop him from going? Why am I so pathetic about all this? Will I ever stop being a doormat?'). Refusing to take responsibility for yourself means you are likely to see yourself as a permanent victim of circumstances rather than as someone taking charge of her life. The late and distinguished philosopher, Isaiah Berlin, described self-responsibility in this way:

> I wish my life and decisions to depend on myself, not on external forces of whatever kind. I wish to be the instrument of my own, not of other men's, acts of will. I wish to be a subject, not an object; to be moved by reasons, by conscious purposes, which are my own, not by causes which affect me, as it were, from outside. I wish to be somebody, not nobody; a doer – deciding, not being decided for, self-directed and not acted upon by external nature or by other men as if I were a thing, or an animal, or a slave incapable of playing a human role, that is, of conceiving goals and policies of my own and realising them. (1998: 203)

While this might be the expressed ideal, in reality, we are all to some extent constrained by external forces. Internal forces which constrain us are our self-defeating ideas and beliefs which, as in the above example, promote intrapersonal conflict and emotional distress and block goal-attainment. Internal constraints are within our power to identify, challenge and change in order to become more self-directed and less self-chained. By dismantling these internal blocks through the methods we have described in this book, you can experience a greater or new-found sense of personal freedom (e.g. 'I'm no longer depressed. I kicked him out for screwing around and gave up this stupid idea that my attractiveness depended on his faithfulness. My attractiveness depends on whether I believe in me, which I now do. The doormat is back where it belongs – outside the front door'). You make the choices for the kind of life you want to lead.

ENLIGHTENED SELF-INTEREST

This is not to be confused with selfishness where you only think about yourself and disregard the interests and desires of others. Enlightened self-interest means putting your own interests first a lot of the time and others' interests, particularly significant others', a close second. The reason that this form of self-interest is enlightened is because if you do not look after yourself, you will not be of much use to yourself or others. For example, if you work consistently long hours you may jeopardize your physical and psychological health, see a decline in your workplace performance and a deterioration in your relationships with your partner, children and friends, and develop a sour disposition. It is important to decide what your priorities are in life (e.g. attain physical fitness, gain more qualifications, have more family outings) and then determine whether your time is actually directed towards achieving these important goals.

Enlightened self-interest also needs to be distinguished from selflessness where you disregard your own interests and concentrate on the concerns of others. Selflessness may be pursued for unhealthy reasons. For example, you believe you are not worthy enough to ever put your own interests first (e.g. 'I'm no good. Only others count'); therefore, your conclusion that your life should be dedicated to the service of others stems from disturbed, self-denigratory thinking. However, if you did believe you had intrinsic worth, no more or no less than others, would you still be as willing to devote your life purely to the service of others?

Enlightened self-interest can mean putting others' interests or needs (e.g. your children's, your infirm parents') before your own because you choose to for non-disturbed reasons (e.g. 'I do want to look after my parents as much as I can, but if the time comes when I can no longer cope, then I will consider a residential home for them'). Whether you put your own or others' interests first some or most of the time, the essence of enlightened self-interest is flexibility: you are responding to the requirements of changing circumstances and situations.

DEVELOP VITALLY ABSORBING INTERESTS

A lot of your time may be taken up with mundane activities that obviously do not excite or absorb you. Therefore, select activities that will fire your imagination and give you a great deal of personal fulfilment (e.g. playing golf, writing poetry, opera going) but without becoming obsessed about them, as this may throw your life out of kilter (e.g. your partner has become a 'golf widow' and is threatening to leave you as 'I never see you any more'). Whatever interests you choose, try not to be deflected from pursuing them by the possible jeers or mockery of others (e.g. 'Brass rubbing! I always knew you were a pervert'). A passion for something (as long as it does not harm yourself or others) forcefully reminds you of the difference between really living and merely existing.

THINK AND ACT FLEXIBLY

Changing circumstances require adaptive responses from us. For example, we are reliably informed that there are no more jobs for life and, therefore, we will have a number of jobs and careers before we retire (even retirement is now seen as full of opportunities and challenges rather than as a sedate, 'winding down' phase of our life). Whatever the circumstances in your life at any given moment, demanding that they should not exist (e.g. 'My partner shouldn't have run off with someone else. What am I to do?'; 'I shouldn't be stuck in this traffic jam when I've got an important meeting to get to') will not make them easier to adjust to or deal with. In all probability, your emotional distress will intensify as you refuse to accept the grim or frustrating reality of events (e.g. depression and withdrawal from social activity; increase in anger).

Research shows that people with good coping skills have learnt to think and act flexibly in the face of adverse events (Kleinke, 1991). When the going gets tough, Dryden and Gordon (1994) suggest, there are two kinds of thinking open to us: adaptive, tough-minded, problem-solving thinking (e.g. 'The shit has hit the fan. I'll clean the fan') and unadaptive, crumble-minded, making-the-going-even-tougher thinking (e.g. 'The shit has hit the fan. Oh God! What am I to do? Can't it be yesterday again? This shouldn't be happening').

Thinking and acting flexibly is also necessary at times with enjoyable events, such as winning a million pounds on the premium bonds. You might believe that to make up for the hard times in your life you are now going to live a highly extravagant lifestyle, but within a couple of years your money is gone and you have to fall back on income support (the hard times have returned). A flexible response to winning the premium bonds would be to enjoy yourself now and invest for the future to provide you with a lifelong income.

DEVELOP REALISTIC EXPECTATIONS

It is highly unlikely we are going to get everything we want in life or avoid everything that might be painful for us. In addition, much valuable time and energy is wasted on striving for the unattainable or what is unrealistic. For example, you might believe that the solution to your problems is to be perfect. How many years have you been trying to be perfect and how many more years will it take before you accept that it is beyond your reach? The human condition is an imperfect one. You may initially agree and then say 'but' . . . which means you do not really agree and therefore will still pursue the holy grail of human perfection. Even if you do some things perfectly (task perfection), this does not make you perfect (self-perfection). Alternatively, you could see yourself as highly effective but fallible, i.e. acknowledge your imperfections and accept you will never be free of all of them, and then focus your energies on striving to reach important but realistic life goals.

LEARN TOLERANCE

Tolerance means you are willing to allow the existence of other opinions and behaviours but without accepting or liking them; if you find someone's opinion or behaviour objectionable, then argue against it but without condemning the person for it. Tolerance allows you and others the right to be wrong and thereby reduces the potential for emotional upsets. Hauck states that when you are angry with others for the opinions they hold, you are acting like a dictator: 'Your anger signifies that you don't like another person's actions and therefore his thoughts, and intend to control both from now on against that person's will' (1980: 70). Remember that you cannot control what others think or how they behave but you can attempt to change some of their views and actions through reasoned debate.

TEACH OTHERS

A key way of deepening your conviction in your new outlook is through teaching others the benefits to be derived from it. It is important not to become dogmatic about your new knowledge (e.g.

'You *have* to be self-accepting; self-esteem does not work'), not to develop a holier-than-thou attitude, not to see yourself as superior (e.g. 'My new way of seeing things in life really emphasizes the myopia of others') nor expect to have all the answers when others find your views unpersuasive or full of flaws (reflecting on their comments can help you to build stronger arguments). Also, when others (e.g. family members or friends) seek your advice, ensure that you really are practising what you preach, otherwise your inconsistencies will become readily apparent (e.g. 'Hey, Mr Hypocrite, why are you getting so angry because I disagree with you? I thought you advocated tolerance of dissenting opinion'). Finally, teaching your children how to be more effective in facing life's challenges can be one of your most enduring legacies to them.

CONCLUSION

We are often told by people that they felt inspired after reading a particular self-help book. Unfortunately, inspiration is not always followed by action or, if it is, the action is not usually sustained (e.g. 'It's very stimulating reading about getting more out of yourself and your life but when it comes to actually doing it, that's another story altogether, isn't it?'). Do not let this happen to you. If this book or any part of it has interested you or even seized your imagination, then commit yourself to and persist with an action plan to achieve your desired goals of increased personal effectiveness. One final thought. You can waste so much time in your life by not going after what you really want that you might believe, at odd moments, you actually have several lives available to you instead of only one. So do not waste any more time – act now!

References

Adair, J. (1988) *Effective Time Management*. London: Pan Books.

Alberti, R. E. and Emmons, M. L. (1970) *Your Perfect Right: A Guide to Assertive Behavior*. San Luis Obispo, CA: Impact.

Alberti, R. E. and Emmons, M. L. (1975) *Stand Up, Speak Out, Talk Back*! New York: Pocket Books.

Arnold, J., Cooper, C. L. and Robertson, I. T. (1995) *Work Psychology: Understanding Human Behaviour in the Workplace*, 2nd edn. London: Pitman Publishing.

Arroba, T. Y. (1978) 'Decision-making style as a function of occupational group, decision content and perceived importance', *Journal of Occupational Psychology*, 51: 219–226.

Atkinson, J. M. (1994) *Coping with Stress at Work*. London: Thorsons.

Barlow, D. H. and Craske, M. G. (1989) *Mastery of Your Anxiety and Panic*. Albany, NY: Graywind Publications.

Beck, A. T. (1976) *Cognitive Therapy and the Emotional Disorders*. New York: International Universities Press.

Beck, A. T., Rush, A. J., Shaw, B. F. and Emery, G. (1979) *Cognitive Therapy of Depression*. New York: Guilford.

Beck, A. T., Emery, G. and Greenberg, R. L. (1985) *Anxiety Disorders and Phobias: A Cognitive Perspective*. New York: Basic Books.

Beck, A. T., Wright, F. D., Newman, C. F. and Liese, B. S. (1993) *Cognitive Therapy of Substance Abuse*. New York: Guilford.

Beck, J. S. (1995) *Cognitive Therapy: Basics and Beyond*. New York: Guilford.

Berlin, I. (1998) 'Two concepts of liberty', in H. Hardy and R. Hausheer, eds, *The Proper Study of Mankind: An Anthology of Essays by Isaiah Berlin*. London: Pimlico.

Bernard, M. E. (1986) *Staying Rational in an Irrational World: Albert Ellis and Rational Emotive Therapy*. Carlton, Australia: McCulloch.

Bernard, M. E. (1993) 'Are your emotions and behaviors helping you or hurting you?', in M. E. Bernard and J. L. Wolfe, eds, *The RET*

Resource Book for Practitioners. New York: The Albert Ellis Institute for Rational Emotive Behaviour Therapy.

Bettelheim, B. (1960) *The Informed Heart.* Glencoe, IL: Free Press.

Bishay, N. R., Tarrier, N., Dolan, M., Beckett, R. and Harwood, S. (1996) 'Morbid jealousy: a cognitive outlook', *Journal of Cognitive Psychotherapy,* 10(1): 9–22.

Blackburn, I. M. and Davidson, K. (1995) *Cognitive Therapy for Depression and Anxiety,* amended. Oxford: Blackwell Scientific Publications.

Booth-Kewley, S. and Friedman, H. S. (1987) 'Psychological predictors of heart disease: a quantitative review', *Psychological Bulletin,* 101, 343–362.

Burns, D. D. (1981) *Feeling Good: The New Mood Therapy.* New York: Signet.

Burns, D. D. (1989) *The Feeling Good Handbook.* New York: William Morrow.

Butler, G. and Hope, T. (1996) *Manage Your Mind.* Oxford: Oxford University Press.

Butler, G. and McManus, F. (2000) *Psychology: A Very Short Introduction,* reissued. Oxford: Oxford University Press.

Chesney, M. A. and Rosenman, R. H. (1985) *Anger and Hostility in Cardiovascular and Behavioral Disorders.* Washington, DC: Hemisphere.

Cormier, W. H. and Cormier, L. S. (1985) *Interviewing Strategies for Helpers: Fundamental Skills and Cognitive Behavioral Interventions,* 2nd edn. Monterey, CA: Brooks/Cole.

Covey, S. R. (1989) *The 7 Habits of Highly Effective People.* New York: Simon & Schuster.

Davis, M., Eshelman, E. R. and McKay, M. (1995) *The Relaxation and Stress Reduction Workbook,* 4th edn. Oakland, CA: New Harbinger Publications.

De Rosario, L. (1995) *Nippon Slaves.* London: Janus.

Dickson, A. (1982) *A Woman in Your Own Right.* London: Quartet.

DiGiuseppe, R. (1995) 'Developing the therapeutic alliance with angry clients', in H. Kassinove, ed., *Anger Disorders: Definition, Diagnosis, and Treatment.* Bristol, PA: Taylor & Francis.

DiMattia, D. J. (1987) *Mind over Myths: Managing Difficult Situations in the Workplace* (cassette recording). New York: Albert Ellis Institute for Rational Emotive Behaviour Therapy.

Downey, M. (1999) *Effective Coaching.* London: Orion Business Books.

Dryden, W. (1990) *Dealing with Anger Problems: Rational-Emotive Therapeutic Interventions.* Sarasota, FL: Professional Resource Exchange.

Dryden, W. (1992) *The Incredible Sulk.* London: Sheldon.

Dryden, W. (1993) *Reflections on Counselling.* London: Whurr.

Dryden, W. (1994a) *Overcoming Guilt.* London: Sheldon.

Dryden, W. (1994b) *Invitation to Rational-Emotive Psychology*. London: Whurr.

Dryden, W. (1994c) *10 Steps to Positive Living*. London: Sheldon.

Dryden, W. (1995) *Facilitating Client Change in Rational Emotive Behaviour Therapy*. London: Whurr.

Dryden, W. (1997) *Overcoming Shame*. London: Sheldon.

Dryden, W. and DiGiuseppe, R. (1990) *A Primer on Rational-Emotive Therapy*. Champaign, IL: Research Press.

Dryden, W. and Gordon, J. (1990) *Think Your Way to Happiness*. London: Sheldon.

Dryden, W. and Gordon, J. (1991) *How to Untangle Your Emotional Knots*. London: Sheldon.

Dryden, W. and Gordon, J. (1993a) *Peak Performance: Become More Effective at Work*. Didcot, Oxfordshire: Mercury Business Books.

Dryden, W. and Gordon, J. (1993b) *Beating the Comfort Trap*. London: Sheldon.

Dryden, W. and Gordon, J. (1994) *How to Cope When the Going Gets Tough*. London: Sheldon.

Dryden, W. and Matweychuk, W. (2000) *Overcoming Your Addictions*. London: Sheldon.

Dryden, W. and Neenan, M. (1995) *A Dictionary of Rational Emotive Behaviour Therapy*. London: Whurr.

Dryden, W., Neenan, M. and Yankura, J. (1999) *Counselling Individuals: A Rational Emotive Behavioural Handbook*, 3rd edn. London: Whurr.

D'Zurilla, T. J. (1990) 'Problem-solving training for effective stress management and prevention', *Journal of Cognitive Psychotherapy*, 4(4): 327–354.

D'Zurilla, T. J. and Nezu, A. M. (2000) *Problem-Solving Therapy*, 2nd edn. New York: Springer.

Ellis, A. (1972) *Executive Leadership: A Rational Approach*. New York: The Albert Ellis Institute for Rational Emotive Behaviour Therapy.

Ellis, A. (1977) *Anger: How to Live With and Without It*. Secaucus, NJ: Citadel Press.

Ellis, A. (1979) (audiocassette) RET and Assertiveness Training. New York: Albert Ellis Institute for Rational Emotive Behaviour Therapy.

Ellis, A. (1980) 'An overview of the clinical theory of rational-emotive therapy', in R. Grieger and J. Boyd, eds, *Rational-Emotive Therapy: A Skills-Based Approach*. New York: Van Nostrand Reinhold.

Ellis, A. (1985) *Overcoming Resistance: Rational-Emotive Therapy with Difficult Clients*. New York: Springer.

Ellis, A. (1994) *Reason and Emotion in Psychotherapy*, revised and updated. New York: Birch Lane Press.

Ellis, A. (1996) 'The treatment of morbid jealousy: a rational emotive behavior therapy approach', *Journal of Cognitive Psychotherapy*, 10(1): 23–33.

Ellis, A. (1999) 'Rational emotive behavior therapy and cognitive behavior therapy for elderly people', *Journal of Rational-Emotive and Cognitive-Behavior Therapy*, 17(1): 5–18.

Ellis, A. and Becker, I. (1982) *A Guide to Personal Happiness*. North Hollywood, CA: Wilshire.

Ellis, A. and Knaus, W. J. (1977). *Overcoming Procrastination*. New York: Albert Ellis Institute for Rational Emotive Behaviour Therapy.

Ellis, A. and MacLaren, C. (1998) *Rational Emotive Behavior Therapy: A Therapist's Guide*. San Luis Obispo, CA: Impact Publishers.

Ellis, A., McInerney, J. F., DiGiuseppe, R. and Yeager, R. J. (1988) *Rational-Emotive Therapy with Alcoholics and Substance Abusers*. New York: Pergamon.

Ellis, A., Sichel, J. L., Yeager, R. J., DiMattia, D. J. and DiGiuseppe, R. (1989) *Rational-Emotive Couples Therapy*. New York: Pergamon.

Ellis, A., Gordon, J., Neenan, M. and Palmer, S. (1997) *Stress Counselling: A Rational Emotive Behaviour Approach*. London: Cassell.

Feltham, C. and Dryden, W. (1993) *Dictionary of Counselling*. London: Whurr.

Fennell, M. J. V. (1997) 'Low self-esteem: a cognitive perspective', *Behavioural and Cognitive Psychotherapy*, 25(1): 1–25.

Fontana, D. (1989) *Managing Stress*. London: BPS and Routledge.

Forsyth, P. (1994) *First Things First*. London: Pitman.

Forward, S. (1997) *Emotional Blackmail*. London: Bantam Books.

Frankl, V. E. (1985) *Man's Search for Meaning*. New York: Washington Square Press. (Originally published in German in 1946.)

Furnham, A. (1996) *The Myths of Management*. London: Whurr.

Gilbert, P. (1989) *Human Nature and Suffering*. Hove: Lawrence Erlbaum Associates.

Gilbert, P. (1997) *Overcoming Depression*. London: Robinson.

Gilbert, P. (1998) 'Shame and humiliation in the treatment of complex cases', in N. Tarrier, A. Wells and G. Haddock, eds, *Treating Complex Cases: The Cognitive Behavioural Therapy Approach*. Chichester: John Wiley.

Gilbert, P. (2000) *Counselling for Depression*, 2nd edn. London: Sage.

Glucksman, M. (1990) (interview) 'Procrastination', *USA Today*, April 17.

Grieger, R. M. (1991) 'Keys to effective RET', in M. E. Bernard, ed., *Using Rational-Emotive Therapy Effectively: A Practitioner's Guide*. New York: Plenum.

Grieger, R. and Boyd, J. (1980) *Rational-Emotive Therapy: A Skills-Based Approach*. New York: Van Nostrand Reinhold.

Gullo, J. M. (1993) 'Visualizing self-created anger', in M. E. Bernard and

J. L. Wolfe, eds, *The RET Resource Book for Practitioners*. New York: Albert Ellis Institute for Rational Emotive Behaviour Therapy.

Hauck, P. (1974) *Depression*. London: Sheldon.

Hauck, P. (1980) *Calm Down*. London: Sheldon.

Hauck, P. (1981a) *Why Be Afraid?* London: Sheldon.

Hauck, P. (1981b) *How to Stand Up for Yourself*. London: Sheldon.

Hauck, P. (1982a) *Jealousy*. London: Sheldon.

Hauck, P. (1982b) *How to Do What You Want to Do*. London: Sheldon.

Hauck, P. (1988) *How to Be Your Own Best Friend*. London: Sheldon.

Hauck, P. A. (1991a) 'RET and the assertive process', in M. E. Bernard, ed., *Using Rational-Emotive Therapy Effectively: A Practitioner's Guide*. New York: Plenum.

Hauck, P. (1991b) *Hold Your Head Up High*. London: Sheldon.

Hitchens, C. (1995) *The Missionary Position: Mother Teresa in Theory and Practice*. London: Verso.

Horney, K. (1950) *Neurosis and Human Growth*. New York: Norton.

Jakubowski, P. and Lange, A. J. (1978) *The Assertive Option*. Champaign, IL: Research Press.

Jones, K. (1998) *Time Management: The Essential Guide to Thinking and Working Smarter*. London: Marshall Publishing.

Kaufman, G. (1996) *The Psychology of Shame*, 2nd edn. New York: Springer.

Kleinke, C. L. (1991) *Coping with Life Challenges*. Pacific Grove, CA: Brooks/Cole.

Knaus, W. J. (1993) 'Overcoming Procrastination', in M. E. Bernard and J. L. Wolfe, eds, *The RET Resource Book for Practitioners*. New York: Albert Ellis Institute for Rational Emotive Behaviour Therapy.

Knaus, W. J. (1998) *Do It Now!*, 2nd edn. New York: John Wiley.

Koch, R. (1997) *The 80–20 Principle*. London: Nicholas Brealey Publishing.

Lakein, A. (1984) *How to Get Control of Your Time and Your Life*. Aldershot, Hants: Gower.

Lange, A. J. and Jakubowski, P. (1976) *Responsible Assertive Behavior: Cognitive/Behavioral Procedures for Trainers*. Champaign, IL: Research Press.

Lazarus, A. A. (1977) 'Towards an egoless state of being', in A. Ellis and R. Grieger, eds, *Handbook of Rational-Emotive Therapy*. New York: Springer.

Lazarus, A. A. and Fay, A. (1975) *I Can If I Want To*. New York: William Morrow.

Lazarus, R. S. (1981) 'The stress coping paradigm', in C. Eisdorfer, D. Cohen, A. Kleinman and P. Maxim, eds, *Theoretical Bases for Psychopathology*. New York: Spectrum.

Lazarus, R. S. (1999) *Stress and Emotion*. London: Free Association Books.

Lazarus, R. S. and Folkman, S. (1984) *Stress, Appraisal and Coping*. New York: Springer.

Leahy, R. L. (1996) *Cognitive Therapy: Basic Principles and Applications*. Northvale, NJ: Jason Aronson Inc.

Leahy, R. L. (1999) 'Strategic self-limitation', *Journal of Cognitive Psychotherapy*, 13(4): 275–293.

Linville, P. W. (1987) 'Self-complexity as a cognitive buffer against stress-related illness and depression', *Journal of Personality and Social Psychology*, 52: 663–676.

Maitland, I. (1999) *Managing Your Time*. London: Institute of Personnel and Development.

Mann, S. (1998) *Psychology Goes to Work*. Oxford: Purple House.

Mansfield, P. (1994) *Why Am I Afraid to Be Assertive?* London: Fount.

Maultsby, M. C., Jr, and Ellis, A. (1974) *Techniques for Using Rational-Emotive Imagery*. New York: Albert Ellis Institute for Rational Emotive Behaviour Therapy.

McKay, M., Davis, M. and Fanning, P. (1997) *Thoughts and Feelings: Taking Control of Your Moods and Your Life*, 2nd edn. Oakland, CA: New Harbinger Publications.

McMahon, G. (2000) 'Time management for stress management practitioners', *Stress News*, the Journal of the International Stress Management Association (UK), 12(2): 7–9.

McMullin, R. E. (1986) *Handbook of Cognitive Therapy Techniques*. New York: Norton.

Meichenbaum, D. (1985) *Stress Inoculation Training*. New York: Pergamon.

Mooney, K. A. and Padesky, C. A. (2000) 'Applying client creativity to recurrent problems: constructing possibilities and tolerating doubt', *Journal of Cognitive Psychotherapy*, 14(2): 149–161.

Neenan, M. and Dryden, W. (1999) *Rational Emotive Behaviour Therapy: Advances in Theory and Practice*. London: Whurr.

Neenan, M. and Dryden, W. (2000) *Essential Rational Emotive Behaviour Therapy*. London: Whurr.

Nelson-Jones, R. (1995) *The Theory and Practice of Counselling*, 2nd edn. London: Cassell.

Newman, C. F. (2000) 'Hypotheticals in cognitive psychotherapy: creative questions, novel answers, and therapeutic change', *Journal of Cognitive Psychotherapy*, 14(2): 135–147.

Northedge, A. (1990) *The Good Study Guide*. Milton Keynes: Open University.

Padesky, C. A. (1993) 'Schema as self-prejudice', *International Cognitive Therapy Newsletter*, 5/6: 16–17.

Padesky, C. A. and Greenberger, D. (1995) *Clinician's Guide to Mind over Mood*. New York: Guilford.

Palmer, S. and Burton, T. (1996) *People Problems at Work*. London: McGraw-Hill.

Palmer, S. and Dryden, W. (1995) *Counselling for Stress Problems*. London: Sage.

Platt, J. J., Prout, M. F. and Metzger, D. S. (1986) 'Interpersonal cognitive problem-solving therapy (ICPS)', in W. Dryden and W. Golden, eds, *Cognitive-Behavioural Approaches to Psychotherapy*. London: Harper & Row.

Quick, J. C., Quick, J. D., Nelson, D. L. and Hurrell Jr., J. J. (1997) *Preventive Stress Management in Organizations*, rev. edn. Washington, DC: American Psychological Association.

Robb, H. B. (1992) 'Why you don't have a "perfect right" to anything', *Journal of Rational-Emotive & Cognitive-Behavior Therapy*, 10(4): 259–270.

Salter, A. (1949) *Conditioned Reflex Therapy*. New York: Farrar, Straus & Giroux.

Sapadin, L. (1997) *It's about Time*. New York: Penguin.

Scott, M. J., Stradling, S. G. and Dryden, W. (1995) *Developing Cognitive-Behavioural Counselling*. London: Sage.

Sheldon, B. (1995) *Cognitive-Behavioural Therapy: Research, Practice and Philosophy*. London: Routledge.

Sichel, J. (1993) 'Values clarification', in M. E. Bernard and J. L. Wolfe, eds, *The RET Resource Book for Practitioners*. New York: Albert Ellis Institute for Rational Emotive Behaviour Therapy.

Smith, M. (1975) *When I Say No, I Feel Guilty*. New York: Dial.

Spivack, G., Platt, J. J. and Shure, M. B. (1976) *The Problem-Solving Approach to Adjustment*. San Francisco, CA: Jossey-Bass.

Terjesen, M. D., DiGiuseppe, R. and Naidich, J. (1997) 'REBT for anger and hostility', in J. Yankura and W. Dryden, eds, *Using REBT with Common Psychological Problems: A Therapist's Casebook*. New York: Springer.

Trower, P., Casey, A. and Dryden, W. (1988) *Cognitive-Behavioural Counselling in Action*. London: Sage.

Walen, S. R., DiGiuseppe, R. and Dryden, W. (1992) *A Practitioner's Guide to Rational-Emotive Therapy*, 2nd edn. New York: Oxford University Press.

Warren, R. and Zgourides, G. D. (1991) *Anxiety Disorders: A Rational-Emotive Perspective*. New York: Pergamon Press.

Wasik, B. (1984) 'Teaching parents effective problem-solving: a handbook for professionals', unpublished manuscript. Chapel Hill: University of North Carolina.

Wessler, R. A. and Wessler, R. L. (1980) *The Principles and Practice of Rational-Emotive Therapy*. San Francisco, CA: Jossey-Bass.

Wolfe, J. L. (1985) 'Women', in A. Ellis and M. E. Bernard, eds, *Clinical Applications of Rational-Emotive Therapy*. New York: Plenum.

Wolpe, J. (1958) *Psychotherapy by Reciprocal Inhibition*. Stanford, CA: Stanford University Press.

Wolpe, J. and Lazarus, A. A. (1966) *Behavior Therapy Techniques*. New York: Pergamon.

Index

Index compiled by Frank Pert